FRANZ LISZT

FRANZ LISZT

BY VICTOR SEROFF

THE MACMILLAN COMPANY

NEW YORK

Library of Congress catalog card number: 66–16106

The Macmillan Company, New York

Collier-Macmillan Canada, Ltd., Toronto, Ontario

Printed in the United States of America

First Printing

Not to the memory of
Countess Marie d'Agoult but to
MARIA
a dear friend who is so
patient and hopeful

PART I
EARLY YEARS

"FRANZ, Franz . . . women will be the ruin of your life." Adam Liszt's last words were lost on his son, then sixteen and still innocent of the world. Franz did not know what his father knew—that the more successful an artist becomes, the more "admirers" he collects, and that musicians, of all artists, hold the greatest fascination for the ladies.

Adam lay on his deathbed, clinging willfully to his vision of a brilliant musical career for his son. And indeed, on the day Adam died and left Franz very much alone, that vision was already unfolding.

Franz Liszt was born on October 22, 1811, in Raiding, a small village in Hungary several hours away from Eisenstadt, where his parents had lived until they had moved to the country two years before. Since 1790, Eisenstadt had been the seat of the famous Esterhazys. One of the richest families in Eastern Europe, they had gained their immense wealth and claim to a royal title in 1687 after the expulsion of the Turks from Hungary. The Princes Esterhazy, traditionally cultured men, did much to develop the arts and encourage artists, musicians in particular. The fame of the family spread across the Continent, and since nearby Vienna had been made the center of music by Mozart, Beethoven, Schubert

Franz Liszt's birthplace in Raiding, Hungary

and Haydn, musicians and music lovers often came to visit the Esterhazy estate.

No Oriental splendor could have surpassed the palace itself, where visitors were provided with such entertainment as daily concerts, German and Italian operas on alternate nights, as well as comic operas, vaudevilles, and Chinese pantomimes for marionettes.

There is no record of exactly what Adam Liszt was doing in Prince Nikolaus Esterhazy's service. His son Franz never dwelled on the background of his family. His parents were of humble origin, his father Hungarian, his mother German. Although the Hungarians who were not peasants claimed to belong to the nobility, and Liszt's name can be traced to the early sixteenth century, Franz Liszt could have justifiably repeated Napoleon's words in reference to himself: *"La Noblesse commence avec moi."*

By the time Franz had reached maturity, he had forgotten

Hungarian, his mother tongue, and spoke French better than German. Although he never learned to write correctly in either French or German, he had nevertheless become a man of the world and a great musician, and that was what counted more than anything else. In fact, Franz had become just what his father would have desired for himself.

Adam's work at the Esterhazy estate had nothing to do with music, but apparently he played the piano well enough to gain encouragement from Joseph Haydn, who served as the royal family's major-domo for the greater part of his life. It has been said, however, that after hearing the pianist Johann Hummel, Mozart's pupil, Adam resigned himself to the violin and guitar, so overwhelmed was he by Hummel's playing. Still, there was no question of Adam's musicality and devotion to the brilliant social and musical activities at the Esterhazys', where he had the chance of hearing and per- haps even meeting—as he later claimed—the foremost Euro- pean musicians of the time. It is only to be expected that when Prince Nikolaus made him steward of his properties in the little village of Raiding, Adam should regard the appoint- ment not as a promotion in reward for his services, but as banishment from the life to which he felt he belonged.

Shortly before he took this position, he married Anna Lager, from Lower Austria. Two years later she gave birth to their son. Since the life of an artist had been denied Adam, he determined to make it the fortune of his son Franz. But the newborn child was so feeble and sickly that he was not expected to live. During his first years he suffered from nerv- ous ailments, resulting in fainting fits. Once he seemed so close to death that the village carpenter was asked to prepare a coffin.

Franz was six before his health had improved enough for Adam to seriously consider teaching him piano, but the boy had shown a remarkable musical aptitude much earlier. As happens with all *Wunderkinds*, Franz was born with such a "musical ear" that long before his feet could touch the floor as he sat on the piano bench he could repeat on the piano melodies he heard his father play. And, as also happens with such children, Franz made such extraordinary progress under his father's tutelage that practicing scales and exercises became his favorite pastime—and he spent far too many hours at it for his health. He lost weight, and the symptoms that had already threatened his life returned. His parents grew alarmed. Music studies had to be temporarily postponed.

But music was not entirely denied him. Often the quiet countryside became alive with a hubbub of bells and cymbals, violins and songs, when the Gypsies passed through the village of Raiding. It was great entertainment for the children to watch them drawing up their carts in the square and setting up their tents, and in the evenings lighting their torches and building a bonfire—and then to watch them dance and listen to their nostalgic songs and dazzling violin playing. These impromptu performances impressed little Franz as much as his father's piano playing—which Adam had taken up again and to which he returned every evening after his daily work was done.

To comfort Franz for having taken him from his favorite toy, the piano, Anna read *Grimm's Fairy Tales* aloud, and the local priest, who taught him reading, writing and arithmetic several times a week, introduced him to the stories of the Bible and the lives of the saints. Here were sown the seeds of Franz's religious feeling, which became most characteristic of him throughout his life.

Gradually his father resumed teaching him, and at the age of nine the boy astonished the family's friends and relatives by playing Ferdinand Ries's *Concerto in E flat major*. Among his listeners was a certain Baron von Braun, a pianist who had also been a *Wunderkind*, but had now lost favor with

The Esterhazy Palace in Eisenstadt

the public. He suggested to Adam that Franz play at his concert in Ödenburg, another small town on the Esterhazy property, a proposal that Adam was only too pleased to accept.

On the day of the concert Franz suffered an attack of a recurrent fever that was referred to as *la fièvre paludéenne*. But his playing of the Ries concerto—and, more important, his own improvisations on well-known melodies—caused such a stir that Adam immediately organized another concert at which Franz was to be the sole performer.

Having passed these two tests, the enterprising father arranged to have his boy play for Prince Esterhazy. This time Franz was a sensation, and the Princess awarded him with a gift of Haydn's "name-book," in which the composer had collected the signatures of all the eminent musicians he knew. The Princess' present was a great honor, but Franz soon lost Haydn's book.

Now the time was ripe, thought Adam, for Franz to seek some financial help for a serious musical education. With this aim in mind, he obtained permission from the Prince to give a concert at the Esterhazy palace in Pressburg. Although Pressburg was still a small provincial town, the Hungarian aristocracy, who patronized concerts, lived there. Adam shrewdly chose a date during the height of the musical season, and he made sure that those who would add social glamour to Franz's recital would be in the audience. The event, which took place on November 26, 1820, marked the beginning of Franz Liszt's musical career.

There is no record of the boy's program, except for a general mention that he scored a great success with his playing of Beethoven, his own improvisations on themes called from the audience, and his sight reading of some extremely difficult bravura passages placed before him on the piano's music rest by several noblemen.

The concert was crowned with the results Adam had hoped for. On learning that the Liszt family was in no position to provide a proper musical education for Franz, the noblemen started a subscription. Counts Apponyi, Amadee, Erdody, Viczay and Szapary headed the list by settling on Franz an income of six hundred Austrian gulden (about three hundred dollars *) a year for six years.

Adam lost no time in resigning his post with Prince Esterhazy. A month later, the Liszts bade farewell to the village of Raiding. The priest shook his head disapprovingly over this venture, and Franz's mother wept as she parted from her friends, but Adam was too exhilarated to delay their departure another moment. And Franz was reading the Scriptures as the stagecoach rumbled on its way to Vienna—the Mecca of musicians.

---

* *The purchasing power of all currencies of the time was, of course, far greater than that of a comparable sum today.*

$\mathcal{E}$NCOURAGED by the initial success of his enterprise, Adam went to see Johann Hummel as soon as he had settled his family in Vienna. He had been so impressed by Hummel's virtuosity that he could not consider anybody else as a teacher for Franz. But Hummel's price for lessons was higher than Adam could afford, so he had to turn to the next choice—Karl Czerny, already known as a pianist and composer.

Adam was proud of Franz's recent success with the Ries concerto, and he expected him to play the piece when he brought him to Czerny. But Franz played Beethoven's *Sonata in A flat major* instead, and according to Adam, the boy's rendition surprised Czerny. The master of piano technique, usually not given to extravagant praise, is supposed to have said, "You may become a greater pianist than any of us."

Czerny agreed to teach Franz at the modest price of one gulden, or about fifty cents, per lesson, but after the first twelve sessions he was so pleased with Franz's rapid progress that from then on he taught him free of charge. Czerny's work with Franz, whom he nicknamed Putzi, amounted to more than lessons—one hour once or twice a week. Franz was to come to Czerny every day, and during their sessions, which lasted from two to three hours, he was to practice under Czerny's watchful eye.

Karl Czerny,
1791–1857

The ten-year-old Franz soon learned that merely "playing" the piano, which was fun, was not enough for a performer and that hard work at every detail of a composition was the prerequisite to mastery. Often he would burst into tears after repeating the same passage a number of times, but Czerny, who had been listening to every note, would calmly light his pipe and tell Franz to start practicing the same passage all over again.

This procedure may have been tedious, but one cannot expect to win a marathon if one's legs are flabby, and Franz obeyed. During the following two years under Czerny, he developed not only the necessary technique and control, but discipline—the foundation required for every artist. For his theoretical musical education, Adam took the boy to Antonio Salieri, who taught him the rudiments of harmony, counterpoint and composition.

Franz resigned himself without much enthusiasm to the grueling demands of his masters, but Adam was impatient with all this "dry" apprenticeship—"dull and uninspired." He wanted his boy to be heard, admired and acclaimed. He succeeded in having Franz play in the homes of the Viennese musical society, and finally news of a new *Wunderkind* reached Ludwig van Beethoven.

It is true that Franz's one cherished desire was to meet the great composer, but whether he actually did so is questionable. According to one story, Herr von Schindler, a close friend of Beethoven's, asked the master not only to attend the recital that Adam was busily organizing for Franz, but to supply a theme on which the boy could improvise. Beethoven is supposed to have come to the concert at the Redoutensaal on April 13, 1823, at which Franz played Hummel's *Concerto in A minor* and a fantasia of his own on the *andante* movement of Beethoven's *Symphony in C minor* for an audience of no less than four thousand. (The storyteller does not mention whether the boy played the concerto with an orchestra or was accompanied by someone on a second piano.) After Franz finished the fantasia, Beethoven is said to have walked to the platform and kissed him on the forehead.

Two bits of evidence cast doubt on this famous story: Beethoven loathed *Wunderkinds* and always refused to hear them, and therefore he certainly never provided Franz with a theme for his improvisations; and Beethoven at that time was already deaf and obviously could not judge Franz's performance.

But Adam was shrewd enough to publicize the "anecdote" so that it was eventually accepted as authentic. And he coupled it with true stories of the audience's enthusiasm and the sensational critical acclaim that Franz's playing had won.

α·χ·
Leprince · 1824

Of equal importance to Adam was the fact that the proceeds from the recital were sufficient to carry him on to his next objective—Paris, where he hoped Franz could complete his musical education at the Conservatory.

As if he were following Leopold Mozart's itinerary of sixty years earlier, when Papa Mozart took the six-year-old Wolfgang on his first European concert tour, Adam arranged for Franz to play in Munich, Stuttgart and Strasbourg on the family's way to France. They arrived in Paris on December 11, 1823, and on the following day father and son went to see Luigi Cherubini about Franz's admission to the Conservatory.

"Here," the twelve-year-old boy is supposed to have said, "is the seat of the mysterious tribunal that consecrates or condemns," and when the two Liszts were ceremoniously ushered into the presence of Cherubini, the director of the Conservatory, Franz fell on his knees to kiss the hand of the man who was omnipotent in the musical life of Paris. But neither this sign of respect—a custom practiced in Hungary toward aristocrats—nor a letter of introduction from Prince Metternich, Austria's foreign minister, could make Cherubini go against the regulations of the Conservatory: No foreigners admitted.

It was an unexpected setback and meant that Franz was denied official recognition in the form of a diploma. But Adam was not to be deterred. Since the main object of entering Franz in the Conservatory was not further study of the piano—both father and son felt that Franz already knew all there was to know about that—but, rather, study of theoretical subjects and composition, Adam consoled himself by trusting his son's creative talent to Ferdinando Paër, the composer of many operas popular in those days and a former

Left: *Liszt as a boy* (*After a drawing by Leprince*)

leader of the Imperial Orchestra, and to Anton Reicha, a famous contemporary musical theorist.

And in order not to let Franz's success in Vienna grow stale, Adam made immediate use of letters to the French aristocracy he had brought from nobles in Austria and Hungary. The Liszts were barely a few weeks in Paris when Franz was invited to play at the house of the Duchesse du Berri, and shortly afterward he played before the Duc d'Orléans. These performances were followed by many others in salons and private houses.

He was hailed everywhere as the eighth wonder of the world. He was compared to Mozart, and his pianism was called equal to, if not superior to, that of Ignaz Moscheles and Hummel, the two acknowledged virtuosi of the day.

But both Adam and Franz believed that his true vocation lay in composing. Although so far Franz had written nothing of importance except a few improvisations and short pieces, Paër insisted on his tackling music for a one-act light opera— and on no less a subject than *Don Sancho or the Castle of Love.*

Young Franz's work on the score was interrupted, however, by Sebastian Erard, the piano manufacturer, who was anxious to introduce his new model of the grand piano. He invited the Liszts to accompany him to London, another objective inspired by Leopold Mozart's program for his own son. But Franz's mother was weary of constant traveling and returned to Austria to stay with her sister in Graz until the planned concert tours were over.

London received Franz even more warmly than Paris. On June 21, 1824, he played at the Argyll Rooms. A week later at the Drury Lane he played Hummel's concerto with George Smart conducting the orchestra, and at Carlton House he was received by King George IV. Then Franz, who was thinking only of the arias he was composing for his opera, was taken back to France for a tour of the principal cities of the French provinces.

In May of the following year, father and son returned to London, and this time Franz played for George IV at Windsor. He also gave a concert at the home of the Duke of Devonshire and two recitals in Manchester. Franz appeared to take it all in stride, as a boy of fourteen would. He unaffectedly showed more pleasure at seeing his favorite dessert on a dinner table set in his honor than at hearing all the praises of his playing: "Oh! Gooseberry pie!" he exclaimed.

Franz's one-act opera, completed after the interruptions of several concert tours, was given on October 17, 1825, at the Grand Opera in Paris. The opera failed, and for one

Paris in the early 1800s

simple reason—Franz was too young to deal with the subject Paër had proposed, too young to illustrate musically the emotions of love and jealousy. The work survived only three performances, and the score was never published. It remained Franz's one and only attempt at an opera.

At the time the boy was depressed, but it is doubtful that this first fiasco in his career could have been responsible. He was simply overworked. The physical and nervous exhaustion of constant traveling and constant performing affected his frail health. He became moody. He longed for solitude he could spend in reading, and he sought solace in prayer. As young as he was, Franz believed that an artist had to fulfill a mission. But the public desired only entertainment, which he compared to the performances of trained dogs—he likened himself to a circus rider. The thought of taking religious orders took a firmer and firmer hold on him, and he spoke about it to his father.

"You belong to art, not to the church," the dumfounded Adam responded, and he took away all the religious books Franz had been reading. But Franz merely acquired new books and read them secretly. He went every morning and evening to church, remaining for hours on his knees, and he fasted several times during the week. His nervous system was so seriously affected that he began to have hallucinations. Then one day Adam found Franz on the floor unconscious. On doctor's advice, he took him to Boulogne-sur-Mer for sea baths.

Gradually, complete rest began to restore Franz's health. But a misfortune far more serious than any so far lay just ahead. Adam contracted typhoid fever. Alone and desperate, Franz called for help from his friends the Erards, but Adam died within a few days, on August 28, 1827, at the age of forty-seven. Franz wrote his mother to join him in Paris and returned to the capital to face life as a man.

 *III*

NOW that he had to take care of his mother and himself, Franz's first concern was to find a place to live, for there was no question in his mind that Paris was to be their permanent home. With the small savings Adam had left, Franz rented and furnished a modest apartment for them at 7-bis rue Montholon. He began to teach piano.

He was already well enough known in Paris to secure a number of pupils. One should not picture him as a struggling young musician such as Mozart had been when he was left alone in Paris and forced to eke out an existence by running to his students from one part of the city to another to give lessons. Franz's pupils were perhaps not particularly endowed with musical talent, but they received him for their lessons in gilded drawing rooms, into which Franz was ceremoniously ushered by footmen. Among his pupils were two daughters of Lord Granville, the British ambassador; the Duchesse du Berri; and several others. Then the Countess de Saint-Cricq, reclining on a chaise longue in the *salon vert* of her family's mansion, asked Franz to take charge of her daughter's musical education.

Caroline was seventeen, a few months older than Franz, a slender brunette with large pensive blue eyes. The two quickly became acquainted. Almost after the first lesson they

Caroline de Saint-Cricq

exchanged their views on literature and the theater—their tastes and opinions seem to have been unusually harmonious. And if Franz began to prolong the one-hour lesson by an extra quarter or half hour, or no longer paid attention to the sonorous strike of the wall clock, it was not because he was following Czerny's example of watching his pupil practice. What they were too shy to say to each other they expressed by exchanging books of poems in which certain lines were heavily underscored.

Caroline's mother was an invalid, but whenever her illness permitted, she liked to assist at these lessons, though she was too discreet to remain in the room after the "first hour" had elapsed. She was aware of the two musicians' growing interest in each other. She liked Franz. Dressed in his close-fitting blue frock coat, with a large Byronic collar, floating tie and buff-colored waistcoat, the slender, romantic youth with long curls down to his shoulders made a favorable impression on the Countess. And she, who was solely concerned with her daughter's happiness, was supposed to have said to her husband: "If they love each other—they are still too young to be aware of it—at least don't prevent them from being happy." His Excellency, the minister of commerce and industry to Charles X, ignored his consort's implication of an eventual marriage between his daughter and a penniless musician.

Soon afterward the Countess died, and Caroline had an extra excuse for seeing Franz more often: In her grief, she claimed, music was her only solace. But Franz was too young and inexperienced in these wiles. He failed to bribe one of the servants, who reported to the Count not only the unusual silence of the piano during the lessons, but also their secret meetings in the evenings.

After one of the lessons Franz was summoned before the Count. What His Excellency had to say was short and to the point. "Monsieur, I owe you many thanks for the lessons you have so conscientiously given my daughter. But they can no longer continue. Before her death, the Countess informed me of your feeling for Mademoiselle Caroline, and no doubt I was wrong in not realizing your intentions, which you must understand as well as I to be impossible.." The Count refrained from telling Franz bluntly that his plebeian heritage as the son of a steward in Esterhazy's little village somewhere in the wilderness of Hungary made the idea of a union with Caroline utterly preposterous. "I might as well inform you," the Count added, concluding the interview, "that my daughter is soon to marry Count d'Artigau, whom I have chosen for her. Monsieur Liszt, farewell. Please be assured of my gratitude and my esteem."

The Count's words cut deeply, wounding more than Franz's pride. Contrary to the Countess' presumption that he and Caroline were still too young to be aware of it, both were very much in love. Caroline became seriously ill, and after her recovery she spoke of becoming a nun, although she was forced eventually to marry the chosen Count d'Artigau.

Franz never forgot Caroline. Sixteen years later, at the age of thirty-three, he made a point of giving a concert in Pau.

A drawing of Liszt in 1832

As he came out on the stage, he saw Caroline, now Countess
d'Artigau, sitting in the second row. On the following day
Liszt visited her at her nearby chateau. Their love had not
been dimmed by the years of separation. "These long years

of waiting have been nothing but a long martyrdom," Caroline whispered to him. "Never grow weary of my memory."

Liszt never saw her again, but in memory of this meeting he composed *Ich möchte hingehn wie das Abendroth*, a song he called the testament of his youth. He also transcribed and dedicated to Caroline two folk songs of Béarn, her native province: *Faribolo Pastour* and *Chanson du Béarn*.

Later, at the age of fifty, he left her in his will a jewel mounted in a ring. But Liszt outlived Caroline, and on learning of her death, he wrote to the woman who succeeded Caroline in his heart:

How could I help withdrawing at once into meditation and prayer? She was one of the purest manifestations of God's blessing upon earth. Her long sufferings, endured with so much Christian sweetness and resignation, had ripened her for heaven. There she entered at last the joy of the Lord—she had no concern with this world, and the Infinite alone was worthy of her heavenly soul. Blessed be God for having recalled her from her earthly exile, and may her intercession obtain for us the grace to remain united to Him.

But at the time Caroline's father closed the door of their home to him, Franz, too, fell desperately ill. It was even reported in the *Étoile* that he had died, and his picture was on sale with the caption: "Franz Liszt, born Raiding, 1811; died Paris, 1828." Those who knew the rumors to be erroneous presumed that he had been stricken with one of the cataleptic fits he had had in his childhood, which had kept him unconscious for as many as two or three days at a time.

Franz refused to appear in public and even stopped teaching. Only his consideration for his mother kept him from entering the church. For eighteen months he remained in a state of depression, during which he was willing to see only one confidant—Christian Urhan, the first violinist of the Opera Orchestra. Those who knew Urhan said that he was a strange, round-shouldered little man who fasted every day until six o'clock, then dined at the Café des Anglais and, by special permission from the Archbishop of Paris, took his seat in the orchestra at the opera, turning his back on the stage so that his eyes, at least, might be averted from evil in the form of a female dancer.

Urhan played for Franz on his viola d'amore, and later they read books together. Gradually Franz began to recover. Lack of funds, the threat of poverty, which has always tempted man to evil, forced him to resume teaching. Once again he went to Mass every day, observed the strictest practices of the Church of Rome, and spent the rest of the time studying a wide choice of subjects. Not having had any schooling, Franz educated himself by reading the works of Hugo, Montaigne, Kant, Lamennais, Senancour, Pascal and others.

Felicien David, the composer, introduced Franz to the doctrine of Claude Saint-Simon, the founder of socialistic teaching in France. Saint-Simon advocated a reorganization of society according to merit rather than breeding—a theory particularly appealing to Franz, because he had only recently begun to recover from his unjust rebuff by the Count de Saint-Cincq.

Franz was also introduced to the Abbé de Lamennais, who spoke of those "tormented by a need to love something and believe in it, and for whom *art* is a religion." Franz saw himself in the Abbé's words—he understood that faith in art is an individual faith, without rational basis, but instinctively sincere, almost involuntary. Without such faith, he realized, talent cannot reveal itself.

Franz plunged even deeper now into studies of the Bible and Homer, Plato, Locke, Byron and Hugo. And when, on the torrid afternoon of July 27, cries of "Down with the Philistines! Long live the new Charter!" heralded the revolu-

A scene from the 1830 Revolution in France

tion of 1830 in France, Franz was impatient for a life of greater promise and beauty to begin. He sketched out a *Revolutionary Symphony* dedicated to Lafayette. But it was music rather than politics that concerned him. From then on he devoted himself to art with the passion of a religious zealot. Art and religion were, indeed, both faiths to Franz.

*Niccolò
Paganini,
1782–1840
(Painting
by Kersting)*

It was at about this time in Franz's spiritual and artistic evolution that three men had major influence on him.

On March 9, 1831, he heard Niccolò Paganini's first concert in Paris, at the Opera. The French debut of the violinist was preceded by a kind of legend. It was said that he had been famous in his native Italy since the early years of the century, that he was at one time a court musician at Lucoa to Elisa Bacciochi, Napoleon's sister, and that he would disappear suddenly from public life only to return to it years later with still greater mastery of his instrument, though he played in his "retirement" only guitar or viola. Now, nearing fifty, he had suddenly decided to show off his art in Germany, France and England.

It was further reported that Paganini suffered from tuberculosis of the larynx, spoke no more than was necessary, and survived on a little soup and camomile tea each day. And that during his concert tours he no longer practiced violin, but remained for hours lying on a sofa, sometimes strumming a mandolin. In order not to reveal the secrets of his own invention he would never play cadenzas—the solo parts in a concerto—during rehearsals with an orchestra, for he wished them to be heard only once and no more. And he was so determined to keep his art to himself that he would not let his compositions be published except on rare occasions, and he only reluctantly agreed to the printing of his *Twenty-four Capricci*.

No other artist's physical appearance was ever in such perfect accord with his art and reputation. Paganini's prominent aquiline nose and sharp dark-brown eyes below a large high forehead framed by locks of raven-black hair made a sardonic, diabolical impression that frightened more than it pleased. His frock coat, his trousers, and what was visible of his shirt collar and tie under his chin were wrinkled as if he had slept in them.

Franz was overwhelmed by Paganini's virtuosity. It opened a vista of endless possibilities for his own instrument; it kindled in him an ambition to transplant Paganini's violin technique to the piano. He realized that his own *Etudes en forme de douze exercises pour piano* (his Opus 1, composed in 1830) was still a work of youth compared to this art. But aside from the purely technical effects of Paganini's playing, Franz was fascinated by the romantic descriptive character of

Paganini's compositions: the distant church bells, military bands, rumbling of thunder and howling winds, all portrayed in musical terms and served in performance by Paganini's dazzling technique.

But the tall, dark, silent Paganini terrified Franz. "A monstrous ego could never be anything but a sad and solitary God," Franz reflected, as he listend to various stories about Paganini. He was supposed to have been taught by the devil, or to have achieved his mysterious powers while in prison, where he was condemned for some twenty years for presumably killing his mistress, or to have learned to play on the one string still left intact on his violin at the end of a concert, a stunt that bewitched his audiences into speechlessness. Yet despite Franz's religious devotion, this diabolical aspect in Paganini's make-up had a paramount influence on Liszt's later compositions—the *Faust Symphony*, the *Mephisto Waltz*, the *Todtentanz*, and the *Sonata d'Après une lecture de Dante*.

Franz had barely recovered from the impact left upon him by Paganini when, during the same winter season of 1830 and 1831, the thirty-year-old composer Hector Berlioz came to Paris. Berlioz was a musical volcano in a perpetual state of eruption. Everything revolutionary that Paganini brought to violin playing Berlioz introduced into his orchestral works, which sometimes required, in addition to a full symphony orchestra, as many as four brass bands. These could produce a blaze and violence of sound that seemed to burst through the walls and raise the ceiling of a concert hall.

Berlioz' debut, in contrast to Paganini's, was a fiasco. He had just received his *Prix de Rome*, and his cantata *The Last Night of Sardanapalus*, which had won him the prize, was to have a public hearing. The composition was meant to be a programmatic work based on a poem that closes with a description of Sardanapalus, who, feeling himself vanquished, sum-

Hector Berlioz, 1803–1869

mons his prettiest slaves and mounts his funeral pyre with them. Berlioz' symphonic interpretation called for a conflagration, the shrieks of the reluctant women, the defiant words of the proud Sardanapalus in the midst of devouring flames, and the crash of the falling palace.

But neither Monsieur Grasset, who was the conductor, nor the orchestra was experienced enough to deal with Berlioz' audacious score. "A hundred thousand curses on musicians who do not count their bars!" a still-furious Berlioz recalled later. "In the score, the horn gives the cue to the kettledrums, the kettledrums to the cymbals, the cymbals to the big drum, and the first sound of the big drum brings the final explosion."

But at the concert the horn made no sound, the kettledrums were afraid to enter, the cymbals and the big drum remained silent while violins and basses carried on their "impotent tremolo," and Berlioz, livid with rage, flung the score into the middle of the orchestra, knocking down two of the music desks. The performance was terminated by a general uproar in orchestra and audience alike. Franz was among those few who were more impressed by the composition than scandalized by its failure.

Before Berlioz' second concert, Franz called on him. The two men were so attracted to each other that an immediate friendship developed, a friendship that increased in warmth and depth with the years. Franz attended a concert at which he heard, besides a more successful repetition of the cantata, the first performance of Berlioz' *Symphonie Fantastique*. He led the enthusiastic applause for the composition and shortly afterward began his own piano version of it, which he used to perform at his own concerts.

The originality and explosive force of Berlioz' works, and the vanity and ambition of their composer, were still overpowering Franz when he met Frederic Chopin.

Chopin's background was similar to Liszt's. He was born in 1810, of a middle-class family of modest means. He had come from Poland, a country where the general mode of living resembled that of Hungary and Austria. Franz had lived there before he came to Paris. Chopin had graduated from a high school in Warsaw, and Franz had had no regular schooling, but there is little doubt that Franz's diligent reading on a variety of subjects made him the superior in general knowledge.

Unlike Franz's revolutionary spirit, which was concerned only with reforms in music, Chopin's was patriotic. Chopin

Frederic Chopin,
1810–1849

was inspired by his exile from the homeland to which he swore he would not return so long as it was occupied by the Russians. Although his youth was spent mostly among aristocrats, from whom he successfully adopted his manners and tastes (though he could not always afford these), Chopin, like Franz and for similar reasons, was rejected by a highborn family—the Wodzinskis—when he asked to marry their daughter in 1835.

As a musician, Chopin was as different from Paganini or Berlioz as night from day. Modest and shy, he shrank from large audiences and noisy demonstrative performances. He preferred to play "at home" for a small circle of intimate friends, and in such a setting his best qualities were revealed. Chopin was not particularly interested in great orchestral works, as was Franz, and he never attempted to write one

himself. He was dedicated exclusively to his own instrument
—the piano.

The general scope of subjects for his compositions—the
preludes, nocturnes, mazurkas, polonaises, waltzes and etudes
—was rather limited, but it sufficed to express the original,
sensitive artist and poet that he was. He enriched piano literature with exquisite works, from which he excluded all imita-
tions of sounds foreign to the instrument.

As a composer, Chopin was already formed, his musical
personality clearly defined, while Franz had not written
enough by 1831 to merit the name of composer. He was
merely a beginner. Of the three men, Paganini and Berlioz
had more influence on Franz than Chopin. It was Franz's
ambition to achieve a virtuosity on the piano such as Paganini's
on the violin, and the overwhelming sound of Berlioz' orchestral works tempted him to make the sound of the piano
reach beyond its natural qualities.

Liszt admired Chopin as a composer. It was reported that
later in his life he said, "I would give all my compositions
for the first eight bars of Chopin's *Etude in C minor.*" And
Chopin so admired Liszt the pianist that he wished he could
steal the other's way of playing his *Etudes.* Chopin dedicated
the *Twelve Etudes* to Liszt.

As pianists, Liszt and Chopin could never have been compared—so different was their art. Chopin had neither the
force nor the brilliance of Liszt's technique, nor his dramatic
delivery. But he did have an exquisite touch, which suited
his works perfectly in the intimate atmosphere he preferred
for his "concerts." He refrained from playing the works of
other composers. Chopin *played* the piano, feeling no need to
astonish or to shock. He sought understanding and sympathy
rather than noisy acclaim. Liszt *performed,* and as a performer, Paganini's showmanship had left its mark upon him.

When he was free from his various social obligations and free from teaching, Chopin composed. Franz, under similar circumstances, practiced the piano in order to reach the greatest possible virtuosity. "My mind and my fingers," he said, "are working like two condemned souls: Beethoven, Hummel, Bach, Mozart, and Weber—are all about me. I study them, meditate, and devour them. In addition, I work four or five hours at exercises—thirds, sixths, octaves, tremolos, repeated notes, etc."

He had withdrawn his *Etudes en forme de douze exercises pour piano* from further publication, and after rewriting them and enlarging six, he had them published again, dedicated to Karl Czerny. These etudes, however, were to undergo another revised edition in 1839 and a final one in 1854, when they became known as the *Douze Etudes d'exécution transcendante.*

PART II
COUNTESS d'AGOULT

$\mathcal{F}$RANZ was a romantic youth, and it would be mis-judging his passionate nature to presume that because his first love affair had ended sadly he was glued to practicing the piano. Whether twenty or well beyond sixty, Franz Liszt had a remarkable way of combining the strict principles of chastity prescribed by the church with the enjoyment of a woman's embrace. Thus after living quietly for two years with his mother in their modest apartment, rarely appearing in public except to visit the Abbé de Lamennais at La Chenaie in Brittany for long theological discussions, Franz spent most of the winter of 1832 at the chateau of Marlioz in the Swiss Alps near Geneva in the company of Countess Adèle Laprunarede, who afterward became the Duchesse de Fleury. Not much has been revealed about their relationship, though it is known that upon his return home Franz suffered no nervous breakdown.

But after tasting Eve's apple, Franz looked with different eyes upon his social life in Paris. The Austrian and British ambassadors, Countess Platen, the Duchess de Duras, the Viscountess de la Rochefoucauld and the Duchess de Ranzan were only a few among the many aristocrats in whose salons Franz was welcome. His piano artistry kept the ladies in rapture, but also his appearance—tall and slender with a

Countess Marie Catherine Sophie d'Agoult

Dantesque profile—seemed to have a devastating effect on his female admirers. That he was well conscious of this can be seen not only from the deliberate attention he paid to his clothes, but from his premeditated dramatic behavior during a performance.

Henry Reeves, in his memoirs, left an account of a recital characteristic of those early days in Liszt's pianistic career. At the end of a long program that included Beethoven's *Moonlight Sonata,* after which he gasped with emotion, Franz proceeded to a final piece of his own. "As the closing strains began," writes Reeves, "I saw Liszt's countenance assume that agony of expression, mingled with radiant smiles of joy, which I never saw in any other human face except in the paintings of Our Saviour by some of the early masters; his hands rushed over the keys, the chair on which I sat shook like a wire, and the whole audience was wrapped with sound, when the hands and frame of the artist suddenly gave way.

He fainted in the arms of the friend who was turning over the pages for him, and we bore him out in a strong fit of hysteria.

"The effect of this scene was really dreadful. The whole room sat breathless with fear, until Hiller [Ferdinand Hiller, one of Liszt's pupils] came forward and announced that Liszt was already restored to consciousness and was comparatively well again. As I handed Madame de Circourt to her carriage we both trembled like poplar leaves, and I tremble scarcely less as I write this."

Franz was too young and inexperienced to toy with the emotions of others without involving his own. As he soon learned, love can be contagious. At a party on May 25, 1833, at the house of Madame la Marquise de Vayer, where he played for the guests, Franz met the Countess d'Agoult. The meeting proved to be even more important to his personal life than his meetings with Chopin and Berlioz had been to his artistic life.

Countess Marie Catherine Sophie d'Agoult was the daughter of a French emigrant, the Viscount de Savigny, and Marie Elizabeth Bethmann, the daughter of the German banker. She was born on December 31, 1805, in Frankfurt-am-Main, but since her father's return to France in 1809 and his purchase of the Chateau de Mortier in Touraine, her childhood had been spent between the two places. Then, after the sudden death of her father in 1818, Marie was sent for her education to the convent of the Sacré-Cœur in Paris.

Marie was not merely a beautiful girl, she was also intelligent and talented. Her knowledge of languages and her charming manners were noticed in aristocratic circles as soon as she had completed her studies and rejoined her mother in Paris. She fell in love with Count August de Lagarde, but their engagement was thwarted, and Marie, still in a daze from her first misfortune and against everyone's advice, married Count Charles d'Agoult.

Marie was twenty-two, and the Count, a former colonel in Napoleon's cavalry, was fifteen years older (not twenty, as some biographers have claimed). They lived in Paris and at the Chateau of Croissy-en-Brie, and they had two children (not three, as has been reported). But Marie's intellectual needs could not be satisfied by her husband and the company he chose, and the marriage ended in estrangement.

Marie was twenty-eight, six years older and much more mature than Franz, when she first met him. She was attracted to the young man not because of his musical performances, but because somehow he reminded her of the many romantic figures that fascinated her in literature—such as ‘Werther, Manfred, Hamlet and Adolphe. Actually, music interested Marie least of all the arts, and after five years of close association with Liszt, she wrote to a friend about Chopin: "He is the only pianist I can listen to not only free of boredom, but with a deep composure." Needless to add, Liszt never knew of this confession.

Like many other women who are not musicians themselves but who "like" music for its soothing effect, Marie was merely disturbed by Liszt's tempestuous performances. Music to her was a prelude to action, not action itself. And if her choice for a companion had to fall on a musician, she most probably would have preferred Frederic Chopin, to whom she actually wrote at about this time. She invited him to visit her and, saying that she was still recovering from an illness, added, "One of your nocturnes would complete my cure." In the postscript she made clear her impatience to see Chopin: "If you cannot come tomorrow, Saturday, if not Saturday, Sunday; etc."

Chopin, quite ill himself at the time, did not accept the invitation. But Franz Liszt, to whom Marie also wrote after their first meeting, did. Without acknowledging her invitation by letter, Franz came to call upon the Countess.

It was not love at first sight. There were several obstacles on both sides. Franz surprised Marie at their first meeting with his air *distrait et inquiet,* like a phantom for whom curfew is about to sound. When he spoke, he spoke impetuously of ideas and judgments that were as strange to Marie as his flamboyant manners.

At the beginning of their relationship his frequent visits were not spent in praise of her beauty and avowals of love, as might have been expected from a young and passionate musician, but in the most serious discussions of such subjects as the destiny of mankind, man's sadness and incertitude, the soul and God. Marie saw clearly the gaps in Franz's education, but the abundance and violence of his ideas were extremely disturbing to her, for they were directed against a society to which the Countess belonged. He revealed to her his hatred of the bourgeois monarchy of Louis Philippe and the power of an aristocracy that was based neither on merit nor virtue. Carried away with ideas he had received from the meetings of the disciples of Saint-Simon, he called for revenge on all iniquities.

"His flashing eyes, his gestures, his smile, now profound and of an infinite sweetness, now caustic, seemed to be intended to provoke me either to contradiction or to intimate assent," Marie recalled later. But there was no coquetry in their conversations. "Between us," she explained, "there was something at once very young and very serious, at once very profound and very naive."

Shortly afterward, Marie went for the summer to her country home at Croissy. There, for the first time, she became conscious of Franz's fascination for her, and after some six weeks of boredom she invited him to join her.

At Croissy Franz first met Marie's children. She felt that

meeting them was disagreeable for him. His manner toward her changed; seeing Marie not as a single, exceptionally attractive young woman but as a mother and wife must have reminded him of the difference in their ages and their lives. "He, who used to be so full of enthusiasm, so eloquent in his talk about the good and the beautiful, so ambitious to elevate his life, to consecrate his great art, so religious in all his thoughts, never spoke of anything now except in tones of irony," Marie commented with regret.

Franz suddenly turned against her. He lauded what he called her "fine life," congratulated her on her brilliant position in society, and admired her royal establishment, the opulence and elegance of everything around her. Marie was bewildered. Was he being sarcastic?

She began to wonder whether she wanted to see him or was afraid of him. Finally his cynical attitude caused an emotional crisis between them during which Marie burst into tears, and Franz fell at her feet and begged for forgiveness. This scene was followed by a complete reconciliation—long walks in the quiet of the Croissy park and discussions of their "past sad lives" and their gratitude to fate for bringing them together. But during the following two years their relationship remained merely a romantic attachment. Although their daily letters, exchanged even when Marie was in Paris, were of an intimate character, they addressed each other as Madame and Monsieur.

According to a sentimental story accepted by most of Liszt's biographers, "the ice was broken, the veil was lifted," when Marie's elder daughter fell gravely ill. For days and nights Franz and Marie were supposed to have remained at the bedside of the child, and when she died, Marie, stricken with grief, leaned on Franz's arm. Their eyes and lips met.

Actually, when the child became ill at the end of October 1834, Franz called several times at her home in Paris but did

not see Marie. After her daughter died in November, she
returned disconsolately to her home in the country. There
she received a letter from Franz saying rather coldly that he
was going to visit the Abbé de Lamennais at La Chenaie. It
was typical of him at a time of crisis to seek comfort in religion. Not only was he not present at the child's death, but
Marie did not hear from him during the following six months.

The death of their daughter caused the final break between
Marie and her husband. Instead of bringing them closer together, it only emphasized their estrangement. Marie's other
daughter was sent off to a *pensionnat*, and Marie herself was
close to nervous collapse when she heard again from Franz,
announcing his intention of leaving France, even Europe,
and expressing hope of seeing her before he left.

This was merely the dramatic outburst of a young lover
so confused in his mind that he could not cope with the
situation. Berlioz advised him against emotional entangle-
ments and the well-known French novelist George Sand, to
whom Franz said that "no one but God was deserving of
love," counseled him to enjoy love's pleasures but not to in-
volve himself seriously. And so, in his most ardent letters to
Marie, he protested that he was not in love, and she, as if
echoing his words, would say that in the solitude and quiet
of the country a mystical mood would take possession of her,
"a kind of desire never to see you again. . . . But I love you
with all my soul." The more they argued against their love,
the more they convinced themselves that they were made
for each other, and at their next meeting Franz, "moved by
the spectacle of her misery," declared that instead of his
leaving France alone they must "fly from the world together."

Liszt's biographers differ in their interpretation of this turn
in their romantic affair. The question is, Who abducted
whom? Did the Countess d'Agoult—nearing thirty, still griev-
ing over the death of her older daughter, willing to desert her

husband and her younger child—seduce the twenty-three-year-old musician and force him to run off with her? Or did Franz, far from being a helpless captive, abduct her?

Franz and Marie eloped for the simple reason that they were expecting a child. Their presence in Paris, therefore, would have been a further complication. Only Franz's mother, whose character was so negligible that she hardly appears in his life at all, was aware of the situation—but she had nothing to say.

According to some reports, their first destination after leaving Paris was Lyon; others point to Geneva. Actually, in May 1835, Franz wrote his mother from Berne—and not Lyon or Geneva: "Surpassing all hope, we arrived here at ten o'clock this morning. . . . Longinus [one of his names for Marie] is here, also her mother. Nothing has been definitely settled as yet, but presumably we will leave here in about four or five days, taking her *femme de chambre* with us. We are both in fairly good spirits, and have no intention whatever of being unhappy. I am well; the Swiss air strengthens my appetite. . . . Adieu; best wishes to Puzzi [his pupil Herman Cohen] and Madame Sand. I will write to you again soon." Madame de Savigny, Marie's mother, who must have accompanied her daughter more for decorum than for any other reason, soon returned to Paris, leaving the couple to their happy solitude.

The two proceeded, as planned, to Geneva, where they settled in an apartment on the rue Tabarzan. They used their retirement in a profitable way. At the Geneva University Franz attended Professor Choisy's philosophy lectures, and their evenings were devoted to reading and discussing literature. Alternate days were reserved for Franz's composing and his piano work.

Marie's ambition was to become a writer. In this respect she was not unlike many young society ladies who kept jour-

*George Sand
(Painting
attributed to
Poterlet)*

nals and drafted long, elaborate letters, hoping thus to develop their literary style, and eventually wrote novels—under
masculine pen names like George Sand, for they were convinced that feminine authorship was an obstacle to recognition. Eventually, Marie published under the pen name of
Daniel Stern, but at this time she was doing articles about
Victor Hugo for a Geneva newspaper and ghostwriting for
Franz (whose own style was never coherent) on the subject
of reforms in practicing music. In articles he sent to the
Gazette Musicale he advocated substituting for concerts of
"hodgepodges that shrivel your ears" programs of works by
Mozart, Beethoven, Berlioz and Chopin.

Soon Marie and Franz were befriended by such illustrious
men as Pyramide de Condole, the botanist; James Fazy, the
politician; Adolphe Pictet, author and scientist; Simonde de

Sismondi, the historian; and Adolphe Denis, geologist and archaeologist. Their stimulating discussions in the apartment on the rue Tabarzan often ended with an impromptu piano performance by Franz, which the neighbors would frequently open their windows to hear.

Away from the social and professional life of Paris, Franz had time to devote himself to composing. While Marie read Shakespeare, Goethe, or Byron to him, he improvised. Once again he was inspired to work. To this early period belong three books of compositions that Franz named the *Album d'un voyageur*. The three books are titled *Impressions et poésies*, *Fleurs mélodiques des Alpes* and *Paraphrases—Trois Aires Suisses*. Almost twenty years later these served Liszt as

A *view of Geneva*
in the
nineteenth century

a foundation for his *Années de pèlerinage*. The first volume is *Première Année: Switzerland* and includes *Chapelle de Guillaume Tell, Au Lac de Wallenstadt, Au bord d'une source, Vallée d'Obermann, Les Cloches de Genève,* and other works. The last-named piece was inspired by the bells of the Cathedral of Saint-Pierre, not far from their apartment. As an epitaph Marie and Franz chose a text from Byron's *Childe Harold:*

> I live not in myself, but I become
> Portion of that around me.

To pacify the prudish Geneva society, which felt scandalized by the couple's arrival in their city, Franz generously offered to teach, free of charge, the talented pupils at the recently opened Conservatory of Music.

The notes he made in his classbook show Franz's own evaluation of his pupils' qualities:

Julie Raffard: Remarkable musical feeling. Very little hands. A brilliant performer.

Amelie Calame: Pretty fingers. Diligent at polishing her work—perhaps unnecessarily. Capable of teaching.

Marie Demallayer: A vicious attitude (if there is an attitude). Extremely ambitious. Mediocre means. Grimaces and contortions.

Ida Milliquet: Geneva artist. Flat and mediocre. Nice appearance at the piano.

Jenny Gambini: Beautiful eyes.

But the solitude for which Marie had hoped was invaded by the "scandalized," notoriously narrow-minded Geneva socialites, who wanted to see the remarkable Liszt in their salons. They ignored his musical talent entirely and gossiped about his conversation, which they found more fatiguing than agreeable because it had been his misfortune to live among literary people who had stuffed him with dangerous doctrines and false notions. And they were shocked by Franz, a plebeian who was capable of presenting his Countess without blushing—for apparently he was proud of his conquest and was taking delight in exhibiting the beautiful aristocratic bird he had caught in his net. They did credit the Countess for his being dressed with better taste than in Paris and for improving his manners.

Marie would have welcomed the first opportunity to leave town. But on December 18, 1835, their daughter was born, and an immediate return to Paris was out of the question.

In registering the birth of Blandine Rachel, Franz gave his own name as her father—Franz Liszt, *musicien*—but her mother he called "Catherine Adelaide Meran, *rentière, âgée vingt-quatre ans*"—thus making Marie only as old as he, per-

Franz Liszt
(*Painting by*
Ary Scheffer)

haps because he was still conscious of their difference in age.

No wonder Marie was comforted when, during the following summer, many friends from her own circle in Paris stopped to visit on their way to Italy. Among these visitors was George Sand, who so far had not met Marie and whose feminine curiosity drew her to appraise this strange union at first hand. Franz and Marie were on a holiday trip in the mountains when Sand arrived in Geneva during the first part of September. After consulting many hotel registers, the enterprising Sand, escorted by Adolphe Pictat, tracked them down in Chamonix.

They all vacationed together for eight happy days, discussing endlessly their theories on every imaginable aspect of music, painting and literature and arriving at harmonious conclusions—otherwise they would not have remained friends for whom this carefree time was unforgettable. Sand brought them the latest news from Paris, one bit of which interested Franz especially. The performances of the pianist Sigismond Thalberg had recently created a sensation there.

V

*T*HERE were several reasons for Marie and Franz's
decision to return to Paris. Their life in Geneva may have
been luxurious for him, but it was far from what she had
been used to. And now that their child had arrived Marie
felt the discomfort of her "exile" more poignantly than ever.
Also her funds were running low and she needed, as a matter
of expediency, to find a solution to their problem. Franz declared that he himself would ask Marie's brother what financial arrangements could be made for her.

Still, the prime reason for Franz's desire to start for Paris
was George Sand's description of Thalberg's success. It
warned him that, because of his long absence, the fickle audiences might forget him. But something else disturbed him,
too. It seemed that Thalberg was treated by society in a different way than the pianists of humbler birth, just as Felix
Mendelssohn's profession was forgiven him because he was
rich and had no need of being paid when he performed at the
homes of aristocrats. And besides, Thalberg was welcomed
in the Parisian salons because his appearance there made up
for the affront a Hungarian Gypsy heartbreaker had inflicted
on society.

Franz's ego was challenged. He was prepared to compete
to defend Marie's pride and his own title of supreme pianist.

Sigismond Thalberg's origin has never been definitively as-
certained. Since his birth in Geneva in 1812 was never regis-
tered, various rumors sprang up about his true parents. According to one story, he was an illegitimate son of Prince
Moritz Dietrichstein and the Baroness von Weltzler of the
family who were friends and patrons of Wolfgang Mozart.
But according to other sources of information, Thalberg was
Prince Metternich's natural son.

Even in his old age, Franz Liszt must have still nursed his
feelings of inferiority to Thalberg, for, brushing aside the
contention that princely blood ran is Sigismond's veins, he
insisted that his rival's father was merely an Englishman.
"Thalberg was very much patronized and glamorized by the
aristocracy, while I was regarded as very uncouth and ill-
bred," Liszt commented resentfully.

Marie and Franz returned to Paris in December 1836 and
took quarters on the ground floor of the Hôtel de France on
the rue Laffitte. George Sand moved to an apartment just
above theirs so that they could share a salon and receive
friends together. Marie had no intention of goading the
gossips, so their home was not open to the "curious" but only
to those intellectuals who were uninquisitive about Marie's
and George Sand's private lives. Among their frequent visitors
were Lamennais, Sainte-Beuve and Eugène Sue. Chopin
brought his friends Hiller and Heinrich Heine and the Polish
poet Adam Mickiewicz, whom Franz called the Dante of the
North. It was at the Hôtel de France that Chopin met George
Sand, who made such an unfavorable first impression on him
that he remarked, "What an antipathetic person, this Sand."
But Sand's name was to be linked with Chopin's for the rest
of his life.

When Franz arrived in Paris that fall, Thalberg had already scored his usual triumph and had left. Therefore the
jousting tournament of which Franz was daydreaming had to

Sigismund Thalberg,
1812–1871

be postponed until the following spring, when Thalberg was expected to return from Vienna. Meanwhile, Franz took part in a concert conducted by Berlioz. At first his reappearance was greeted coolly by the audience, but after his brilliant performance of Berlioz' *Symphonie Fantastique* in his own piano arrangement, his listeners were aroused once again. And when Berlioz had finished conducting his *Marche au Supplice*, Franz, not yet satisfied with his own success, returned to the piano and played his version of it with an effect that surpassed the brilliant orchestral execution of the piece. One can easily imagine the Parisians' excited anticipation of the day of combat between the two piano titans.

Three months later, Thalberg played his fantasies on *God Save the King* and on Rossini's *Moses* in the hall of the Conservatory for an audience of about four hundred. Franz performed at the Grand Opera before at least five times as many listeners. He played Weber's *Concertstück*, Beethoven's *Hammerklavier Sonata*, and his own fantasia on Pacini's *Niobe*.

And finally, on March 31, 1837, both artists played in Princess Belgiojoso's salon. Thalberg's outstanding pianistic qualities were indisputable: his *jeu perlé*, a light, silvery percussion playing of rapid passages; a singing tone both in his legato playing and when sustained by a pedal; and a complete control of the instrument, so that his demeanor at the piano was always quiet and dignified.

But in this unique rivalry Chopin took Liszt's side. "Thalberg plays beautifully," he remarked, "but he is not my man. He plays both *forte* and *piano* with the pedal and not with his hands. He spans ten notes as easily as I do eight. And he wears diamond studs in his shirt." And the general verdict that "Thalberg is the best pianist in the world, but there is only one Liszt" closed the competition.

Having proved his supremacy as a pianist, Franz was anxious to return to his retirement and devote himself to composing. Marie was not well enough to leave Paris, but he accepted George Sand's invitation and went by himself to Nohant, Sand's summer home near a small village in the middle of Berry.

The two-story house in the style of Louis XVI, to which his grand piano was transported at great expense, was just what Franz wanted for his solitude. From his window he could see a garden full of flowers, a small wood strewn with myrtles, and luxuriant fields and meadows with browsing sheep where he could take long walks.

George Sand had planned to make Nohant a home where artists could work undisturbed away from large cities. This remained only a daydream, but she did manage to have the house full of guests—poets, writers, painters and musicians—who, even if they did not do much work, enjoyed her hospitality and a very pleasant vacation.

Sand was a prolific writer. During her somewhat turbulent life she produced over one hundred volumes. She was extraordinarily disciplined where her writing was concerned, but she worked at rather odd hours—from midnight until five in the morning. Franz's desk was placed in her working room so that the two retired there after everyone else had gone to bed.

Franz was immersed in his transcriptions of Beethoven's symphonies, while Sand, at another table, was finishing one of her novels. They shared the same box of cigars and drank innumerable cups of coffee. And although Liszt said later, "We had an intellectual life the memory of whose moments I have kept religiously in my heart," he must have referred in general to his sojourn at Nohant and not to his nightly *tête-à-tête* with Sand. For it would be underestimating the lady to infer that she could have missed such an opportunity for romance.

When Marie finally joined Franz, she was at first willing

George Sand's château at Nohant

to put up with these "work sessions," but after several weeks of them she reminded him of their plan to go to Italy, and they departed on their *années de pèlerinage*, as Franz named these years. Franz may have kept the memory religiously in his heart, but the friendship of the two women was never again the same.

Franz and Marie had not been to Italy before, and they were so enchanted by the beauty of the Italian lakes that they did not hurry to reach Como, the first stop on their itinerary. After spending some time at Lake Maggiore, they arrived in Bellaggio, on Lake Como. The oleanders were in bloom, figs were ripening in the sun, and the scent of magnolias bathed the air. There was no need to go any farther, at least for a while. They rented the Villa Melzi, with its beautiful garden, and at last they found their long-desired *solitude à deux*. "What is there in all the world," Marie wrote in her journal on September 6, 1837, "but contemplation, work and love?"

And indeed, Franz surprised Marie, who had anxiously watched him waste himself on idle distractions in Paris, Geneva, and again in Paris. She was astonished to find him constantly in a good mood and happy. At an age when everything impels a man to action, when excitement and variety of impression are almost a condition of existence for an artist, Franz seems to have been satisfied with a bad piano, a few books, and serious conversations with the woman he loved.

Together they read Dante's *Divine Comedy*. Dante was among Liszt's favorite poets, and even at that time in Bellaggio he must have contemplated composing a major work such as his *Dante Symphony*, completed almost twenty years later. Marie's readings of Dante aloud led Franz to improvise and later to write the *Fantaisie quasi sonata*, subtitled, *d'Après une lecture de Dante*. He revised the fantasy some ten years later and it was published in 1848. This remarkable piece has the glare and dazzle of romantic art, but it really requires an interpreter with Lisztian technique and imagination.

This was Franz's first product in a long list of compositions to fill the second album of his "years of pilgrimage," *Années de pèlerinage: Italy*. Marie's second product was another girl, born on November 25, 1837. In memory of Como they called her Cosima and she later became Richard Wagner's wife.

But Franz's frame of mind was too virtuous to last. The duality of his nature—one half seeking solitude for his work, the other needing a turbulent public life, acclaim and glory —was his strongest trait. The joys of self-gratification, the excitements of conquest, and the amusements of social life were the obstacles that stood in the way of his serious work all his life. He was too weak to resist them.

The discord within Franz was reflected in his relationship with Marie. Marie fell in love with him. She sought an artist, but found a virtuoso; she desired to see in Franz the epitome of a master and not merely an unusual talent. Franz fell in love with her not only because of her beauty, but because of her title. He was flattered that a woman with her social position had deserted her family for him and, defying convention, not only lived with him but became the mother of his children. Marie was far more mature than Franz and had a stronger and more disciplined character. However, she did not manage always to keep a firm grip on him, and she was not successful in her guidance.

" 'You ought to make better use of your time—work, learn, take exercise, etc.,' " Franz quoted Marie. "Often she scolded me, in her own way, for my indolence, my indifference; and her words depressed me. Work? Make use of my time? But what can I do with my time? What can I and ought I to work at? Reflect as I will, grope as I will, I do not feel a vocation within me, nor can I discover one outside me. . . . I have all the *amour-propre* and all the pride of a high destiny; what

*Liszt with his friends. Left to right: Alexander Dumas,
Victor Hugo, George Sand, Paganini, Gioacchino Rossini,
and Countess d'Agoult*

I have not is the calm and sustained conviction of such a
destiny. . . . There is a storm in the air, and my nerves are
horribly irritated. I feel I am a prey. I feel an eagle's claws
tearing at my breast; my tongue is dried up. Two opposed
forces are at war within me; one of them impels me toward
the immensities of infinite space, high ever higher, beyond all
suns and all heavens; the other draws me toward the lowest,
darkest regions of calm, of death, of annihilation. And I remain nailed to my chair, equally wretched about my strength
and my weakness, not knowing what will become of me.
Why have I squandered my fine gifts for some paltry fem-

inine idols, that must of necessity laugh at me for it? There have been many days in which I have not written a single line. I sometimes suffer bitterly for my inability to handle speech as I can the keys of my piano. It would be gratifying to be able to express nobly, simply and powerfully what I have thus felt in certain hours of my life. . . . I am like the she-wolf in Dante '. . . that in its leanness seemed to be burdened with every desire.' "

Franz wrote this at the age of twenty-seven in a journal that he occasionally kept. What he understood about himself then remained valid throughout his life. He was only too conscious of what was wrong with him, and when he could not find an escape in religion, to which he turned more and more often as he grew older, he simply resigned himself to his weakness.

Milan, the center of musical activities in Italy, was too close to Como to keep Franz at his writing desk. He was well aware that his piano playing was his best introduction. Once in Milan, he walked into the shop of the music publisher Riccordi, sat at the piano and played with such astounding mastery that Riccordi rushed out of his office exclaiming, "This must be Liszt or the Devil!" Thereupon he offered Franz his villa in the Brianza, his horses and carriage and his box at La Scala Opera House, and he opened to him the doors of his famous library of fifteen hundred musical scores, all to be used at Franz's discretion.

Also, Riccordi set out immediately to organize a concert and to invite a select audience. The taste of the Milanese was still rather primitive, and the audience's behavior was rather singular: During the performance the fashionable society in the loges continued greeting friends and exchanging the latest gossip *pleno voce*, while in the rest of the house the listeners would join the performer by whistling or singing as soon as they recognized the melodies.

Franz's playing caused astonishment, but not real interest until he launched forth with the old juggler's trick of improvising on themes chosen by the audience. For this purpose a silver urn, "from the hand of one of the best pupils of Benvenuto Cellini," according to Franz, was placed in the lobby, and listeners were asked to drop their suggestions in it.

As long as the themes were taken from Bellini's and Donizetti's operas, Liszt accepted the challenge quite seriously, but when he found notes requesting him to improvise on such subjects as the Milan Cathedral, a railroad, or the question "Is it better to be married or remain a bachelor?" he sadly thought again how much a pianist's trade is like that of a buffoon.

He was, however, rewarded by serious audiences at the homes of Princess Belgiojoso, Countess Samoyloff, Countess Maffei and Rossini, who had just retired to Milan. Franz played for him his own arrangements of the overture to Rossini's opera *William Tell* and of the dozen songs of Rossini's *Soirées musicales*. He was also the first to play Beethoven's sonatas in Italy.

Upon his return to Bellaggio, Franz complained about the Milanese society to Marie, who considered the Italian aristocracy dull and lacking in culture. He claimed that his heart had been eaten by anxiety over his work, that he had been wasting himself on the public—although he knew that it was as bad for him as tobacco and coffee, he could not do without it.

Marie had recovered sufficiently from their child's birth so that they could proceed to Venice, the next stop on their journey.

VI

*N*OT every beautiful environment is inspiring to creative work. If Liszt had composed while in Venice, he would have done so despite the bewitching beauty of that city.

Marie did not scold Franz for wasting his time there. Like lovers on a honeymoon they took rides in gondolas and admired the old palaces, which looked as if they were made of lace. They visited the churches, monuments and narrow winding streets, and they crossed and recrossed the bridges over the canals in search of still other enchanting spectacles.

Marie did not even object to accepting invitations to sumptuous and lively *soirées* given by the Venetian aristocrats in their *palazzos*. Franz was very gracious and played his *Grand Galop chromatique*, one of the *Etudes*, which, because of its general appeal, had become a great warhorse in his concert programs, and his *Grande Fantaisie dramatique*, subtitled *Reminiscences des "Huguenots" de Meyerbeer*, which he began in 1837 and completed at about this time. It was the only composition he dedicated to Marie. She considered it the best of his works based on themes by another composer.

Not until much later, in 1861, did Franz's Venetian experience bear fruit when he added to the *Années de pèlerinage:*

Italy, under the title of *Venezia e Napoli,* three short compositions: *Gondoliera, Canzone,* and *Tarantella.*

There is no record of how long they planned to remain in Venice, but in April, Franz suddenly interrupted their happy stay there. He had read in a German newspaper about the devastation in Hungary caused by the flooding of the Danube. Though he had only a vague recollection of his native land— Paris and France were his home—he was so distressed by this misfortune, he said, that he felt it was his duty as a Hungarian to do his share to assist his countrymen. Saying to Marie that he would give a concert or two for their benefit and would return within a week, Franz left for Vienna.

Vienna was at the center of musical life in Europe. Since Mozart, Beethoven and Schubert had made the city their home, a great many musicians from all over Europe were drawn there by the outstanding opera and concert performances and by the musical sophistication of the audiences. There at last Franz felt he could safely perform the German classics without being criticized for it. He met Clara Wieck, Robert Schumann's future wife, who showed him Schumann's latest compositions, including the *Carnival,* which Liszt immediately added to his programs. And instead of one week with two recitals, he remained in Vienna a whole month, giving a total of ten.

But his prolonged stay was not solely because of patriotism, although he did donate twenty-five thousand gulden to the Hungarian relief. Franz was intoxicated by his success and relished the life that success offered him. But there was still one object closer to his heart than his work on behalf of the unfortunate Hungarians.

Vienna was Thalberg's domain, and Franz aimed to wrest it from his rival. This time he did not seek open combat with Thalberg, but he believed that if two recitals could not convince the Viennese of his superiority, ten would. And he was

*The Augarten
in Vienna*

also determined to be accepted not only by the Viennese
aristocracy, but by the court of Emperor Ferdinand and
Empress Anna Carolina, which could bestow on him the
coveted title of "a royally and imperially licensed artist."

The desire was thwarted, however, by Count Sedlnitzky,
the chief of police, who reported to the Empress that Liszt
had attracted unfavorable attention to himself in Paris because of his association with George Sand, Lamennais and
other persons "of dubious repute" and because of the scandal
caused by his "elopement" with a certain Countess d'Agoult.
But Count Sedlnitzky conceded that he had no cause to
suspect Liszt of supporting revolutionary (*i.e.*, socialistic)
views while in Italy or Vienna. In closing his report the
Count added his own opinion of Liszt: "He appears to me
simply as a vain and frivolous young man who affects the
eccentric manners of the young Frenchmen of the day, but
good-natured and, apart from his merits as an artist, of no
significance."

Franz had to be content with only one invitation to play at the court, but he had added a new string of titled admirers from the frigid circles of Viennese society to those already collected in Milan and Venice. It seemed that he was more impressed by the "brilliant business" he was doing, by the admiring crowds always in his room, than by the praise of musicians like Clara Wieck, who wrote to Schumann: "He can be compared to no other virtuoso. He is the only one of his kind. He arouses fright and astonishment, though he is a very lovable artist. His attitude at the piano cannot be described, his passion knows no limits, and he has great spirit."

Despite Marie's letters asking him to return because she was not feeling well, Franz could not tear himself away from the flattery of his patrician company. "Why did I not leave here after the first few days?" he replied to Marie. "Or rather, why did I ever decide to come here? I assure you, my good, my only Marie, I do not think that I have done wrong. I suffer as you do, less nobly but just as deeply. I still feel myself worthy of your love, your compassion." Yet he prolonged his stay by another two weeks before returning to his family in Venice.

Marie had no illusions about his Viennese journey, and the more he talked to her about it, the more he confirmed her worst fears. She realized that he had stayed so long away not because of patriotism, but for the sake of salon success, for newspaper glory and invitations from princesses—"for such small motives." Marie was very much saddened.

She noticed a definite change in Franz. From his descriptions of the parties he had attended and those he had given himself, Marie gathered that he had not donated all the money he earned to the Hungarians. He was elegantly dressed and was no longer embarrassed by his lapses in taste and behavior, but reasoned about them philosophically. He spoke of the necessities of his "position" and was secretly pleased

with his exploits with women, which he nonchalantly re-
counted to Marie until she had had enough of it and called
him a *Don Juan parvenu.*

He revealed clearly that his success and the life in Vienna
had put an end, at least temporarily, to his desire for "mystical contemplation" and "the slow gestation of great original
works"—and to his love for Marie. He considered his Viennese
experiment to be the beginning of a brilliant pianistic career
that would take him on tours throughout Europe for months
and months at a time without Marie's company. And as if
he suddenly felt that flaunting their relationship might harm
his "position," Franz hinted to Marie that she should return
to Paris alone to resume her place in society. In his cynicism
he even suggested that she take a certain Theodore as a lover.

Obviously he failed to consider Marie's feelings. She still
loved him as much as ever and was not yet ready to accept
his hint. "Let us try again," she suggested, as so many women
have said and will say under similar circumstances.

After a few days in Venice, they went to Lugano for the
summer, planning afterward to journey south to Genoa. But
Marie was still convalescing slowly from her illness, so Franz
went ahead by himself. When she joined him later she was
shocked to see that after giving a concert he had immediately
rented a magnificent villa, bought horses and a carriage, and
was once again in a turmoil of social life. She managed to
persuade him to move on to Florence and Rome, where she
believed the art treasures would prevail over his thirst for acclaim and amusement.

Raphael and Michelangelo, Liszt declared, did help him to
understand Mozart and Beethoven better. The Colosseum
and the Campo Santo of Pisa were no longer strange to him
when he recalled Berlioz' *Symphonie Fantastique* and his
Requiem. When he heard the choir of the Sistine Chapel
sing Palestrina, Allegri and Vittoria, the music somehow har-

monized with his impressions of the works of Giovanni Pisano
and Fra Angelico. Some ten years later, the Campo Santo
and Orcagna's fresco of the *Last Judgment* inspired his *Todtentanz*—variations on Berlioz' *Dies Irae* for piano and orchestra, which he worked on for six years but which was not
performed until he was almost seventy.

His religious feelings, dormant of necessity during his
worldly existence, were awakened not only by the masterpieces in the galleries of Florence and Rome but by the
resplendent church ceremonies he attended and the sacred
music he heard. In Rome, Marie and Franz lived in the Via
delle Purificazione, almost symbolic of his new life.

Raphael's picture in the Vatican led to his *Sposalizio*, and
Michelangelo's Tomb of Giuliano de' Medici in the Cappela
Medici in Florence, led to his *Il Penseroso*—short piano pieces
that he added to the list of his compositions in the *Années de
pèlerinage*. At the same time he set three *Petrarch Sonnets*,
at first as songs and later as short piano pieces, in typical
Lisztian style, akin to that of his *Fantaisie quasi sonata* only
on a much smaller scale. This creative period in Rome was
marked also by tolerable contentment with Marie, who at
about this time gave birth to their son Daniel.

But it was not destined to last much longer. Franz Liszt
was no model for a husband and even less for a father. There
is no evidence that he had much affection for his children
when they were young. In the evenings he would sometimes
play for Blandine, his elder daughter, Schumann's *Scenes
from Childhood*, but he preferred to amuse himself with his
greyhound. And just as he had left Marie and had gone to
Milan after Cosima was born, he now announced his departure for Vienna.

He had read in the papers that the French had failed in
their public subscription for a monument to Beethoven in
Bonn, and that the collected sum of four hundred and

twenty-four francs and nine centimes (approximately three hundred and fifty dollars) was considered too insignificant for the sponsors to go on with their project. Franz was indignant. He wrote immediately to his friend Lorenzo Bartolini, the sculptor, in Florence, asking him the price for such a monument and the length of time needed to complete it. Bartolini required two years and sixty thousand francs for the marble. Without a second thought Franz informed the Beethoven Memorial Committee in Bonn that he would guarantee the necessary funds on one condition—that Bartolini and no one else be commissioned to do the work.

Sixty thousand francs seemed like a large sum, even to Marie, but Franz assured her that three concerts—one each in Vienna, Paris and London—would suffice. The plan sounded familiar—Marie still remembered the "two concerts in one week" that had taken Franz to Vienna the year before.

The concert tour was to begin at the end of the summer; which they spent first in Lucca, then in Pisa, and finally in San Rossore, a fishing village on the seashore. It appeared that they were trying to escape the heat of the Italian sun, but actually it was the crisis in their four-year-old relationship that made Marie and Franz so restless.

They avoided quarrels. Silence substituted for explanation and argument. Reason, Marie thought, when it intervenes so late in a desperate situation, helps not to cure the ill but only to sound its depth. She buried her grief so deeply in her heart that even Franz could not hear her weeping. After four years they had reached a dead end. Franz tried to console her. He argued that their separation was going to be just temporary, that she should not accompany him because she could not endure so much traveling, that she had to take care of the children. And once he had broached this subject he suggested that she settle in Paris with her family.

"My family?" Marie asked, aghast. "Have I one now?"

*Cosima and
Blandine Liszt
(Pencil drawing
done in 1846)*

Would my grown-up daughter accept me?" And, breaking
down, she said, "My only vocation was my love for you, the
desire to please you."

Franz was already too far away from her in his thoughts
and plans to be willing to prop up their "marriage." Like the
Tower of Pisa it had striven to be lofty and upright, but the
earth had crumbled beneath it.

They parted in Florence. Marie, with their three children,
went back to Paris; Franz went to Vienna. They corresponded
and even met occasionally, but this was the end of their happy
life together.

The warning of Franz's father as he lay dying should have
been addressed to Marie, the first woman to suffer from a
close association with his son. Franz only profited by Marie's
love—everything he composed in this short period was solely
due to her. Not the one single composition, but all his
works written at that time should have been dedicated to
Countess Marie d'Agoult.

VII

*W*HEN Liszt arrived in Vienna, his manager informed him that he had arranged for not one recital, as Franz had told Marie he was planning, but six—all of which were sold out. In addition, six hundred people had subscribed for seats for any other concerts he might give.

On his long journey to Vienna, Liszt had caught a bad cold, but it did not prevent him from scoring a great success before an audience of two thousand, including the Dowager Empress in the royal box.

Always aware of the general public's desire to be impressed by his virtuosity before anything else, Franz's programs consisted of popular and brilliant pieces that could not fail to catch fire. He played his transcriptions of the *William Tell Overture*, Beethoven's *Pastoral Symphony*, Schubert's *Ave Maria* and some selections from his *Etudes Transcendantes* or from the *Années de pèlerinage*. And with his dazzling performances of the *Tarantella* from *Venezia e Napoli* and the *Grand Galop chromatique* he dealt the final *coup de grace* to an already dizzy audience.

In private homes, however, where his listeners were more interested in "serious" music, Liszt not only played Bach, Scarlatti and Beethoven, but also what was contemporary at that time—the works of Chopin and Schumann. He was the first pianist to play everything from memory, the first to inaugurate recitals—that is to say, entire piano performances by just one musician—and the first to devote a whole recital to the works of one composer: Bach, or Beethoven, or, of course, Liszt.

The receipts from his concerts must have provided him with a sizable portion of the sixty thousand francs he had guaranteed for the Beethoven monument in Bonn, but he was in no hurry to continue his tour immediately with this aim in mind. His triumph in Vienna was so widespread that a Hungarian delegation came to the city to invite him to Budapest. Liszt was anxious to visit his native country, and on the way to Budapest he gave a concert in Pressburg, where, at the age of twelve, he had begun his career. Then he had been a boy whose talent his father was showing off to gain financial support for his son's education from the wealthy Hungarians. Now Liszt returned as an illustrious and acclaimed celebrity.

On Christmas Eve, 1838, two days after the concert, he arrived in Budapest. He was the guest of Count Leo Festetics, and a series of banquets and *soirées* was given in his honor. The greatest of these occasions took place after a concert that he closed with his own arrangement of the *Rakoczy March*— or, as he called it, the *Marseillaise aristocratique hongroise*. At a ceremony after the performance, six Hungarian noblemen presented him with a sword inlaid with jewels, and a torchlight procession with a military band escorted him home.

Outside of Hungary, this unprecedented expression of respect for a pianist merely caused mirth, and the reports were accompanied by the following quatrain:

> Among all warriors, Liszt alone is above reproach,
> For despite his grand saber, one knows that this hero
> Did not conquer anything but the "double croches"
> And killed nothing but pianos.

But to come away from his native land with only a single trophy—a saber that would hardly be appropriate dangling from his side on a concert stage—was disappointing for Liszt. While in Vienna he had launched on a campaign to get the Hungarians to bestow a title upon him. There was a question about the arms he should assume. A lyre, a harp or a roll of manuscript would have looked absurd on a coat of arms. Everyone agreed that the image of an owl would have been more appropriate.

Liszt immediately wrote to Marie for her advice. A well-bred woman who did not need to have the fact publicly advertised, Marie was always amazed by Liszt's craving for acceptance by "the most elegant and the most aristocratic society," as he never failed to report to her. But by coincidence his letter to Marie crossed one from her, telling him that she had bought him a pin for his cravat with the image of an owl on it. Liszt had to be contented with the pin, for the dreamer's scheme of receiving a noble title came to nothing.

Nothing, however, prevented Liszt from behaving like a nobleman. He reported to Marie that when he entered his box at the Hungarian Theater in Budapest before a performance of Beethoven's *Fidelio* the whole audience greeted him with a standing ovation, which he "acknowledged three times, no more, no less, in the style of a king." He gave dinners with twenty-two courses, and suppers of forty-five for his "titled" admirers, and in his "position" he felt it necessary to "ruin himself with the tailors."

After Budapest he went to Prague, which was renowned for its good taste in music. There his usual programs were received less enthusiastically, but he cheerfully dispensed with the opinions of the "musical purists," so long as the "feminine and aristocratic public" voiced its approval.

In Leipzig, the next stop on his tour of European cities,

he fared worse. There he found no aristocrats to hobnob with, and the "bourgeois" Leipzigers suspected him as a charlatan. The failure of his concert sent him to bed sick. If it had not been for Felix Mendelssohn, who organized an orchestral and choral concert in his honor at which Liszt, his pupil Ferdinand Hiller and Mendelssohn played Bach's *Concerto for Three Pianos*, there is no telling how long Liszt would have remained in bed nursing his hurt vanity.

Having somewhat re-established his reputation with the Leipzigers, he returned to Paris, where after a separation of almost two years he rejoined Marie. During a month together the same old incompatibility became only too apparent. Marie was bored with the titled "personages" Liszt bragged of as his close friends, his triumphs and escapades with women and his pride in his expensive dandy's wardrobe. She still believed he was wasting himself on trifles while he should have been composing, still believed he needed seclusion for his work and not the life he was leading. But Liszt paid no attention to her. He was on his way to London, where even greater names in society were to be conquered. He arrived there early in May 1840.

According to his usual routine, he started his London season by visiting and playing at the homes of Lady Blessington, the Count d'Orday, and Lord Burghersh, friend of Rossini, where he met Louis Bonaparte and Lord Chesterfield. He played at the Royal Philharmonic concerts on May 11, June 8, and June 14, 1840, but the *Musical Journal* remarked: "Liszt has been presented by the Royal Philharmonic Society with a beautiful silver breakfast service for doing that which would cause every young student to receive a severe reprimand—viz., thumping and partially destroying two very fine pianofortes."

The term "recital," which Liszt gave to his concerts, bewildered the English. "How can anyone recite upon a piano?"

Right: *Franz Liszt wearing the Order of the Golden Spur (After a painting by Kaulbach)*

Below: *A caricature of the grand warrior of the keyboard*

they asked. Or was it his singular behavior that forewarned his audiences? "After performing a piece on his program," a listener said, "Liszt would leave the platform and, descending into the body of the hall, where the benches were so arranged as to allow free locomotion, would move about among his auditors and converse with his friends, with the gracious condescension of a prince, until he felt disposed to return to the piano."

And to make the most favorable impression on English society, he asked Marie to send him immediately from Paris his fur-trimmed Hungarian overcoat, his white dressing gown, also fur-trimmed, and his gray jacket. But with all this ammunition, and his undisputably winning personality, he succeeded only in making the British regret his chosen profession: "What a misfortune to let such a man be a piano player!" the snobs all agreed.

His concerts were so poorly attended that on one occasion he invited his entire audience—only ten people—to his hotel, where he played his program for them after a sumptuous dinner. Scheduled performances in the provinces were preceded by rumors about his relationship with Marie, so even the curious music lover did not turn out to see him. Liszt was forced to cancel his contract and to admit that his visit to England had been a total fiasco. A year later he returned to play at the Royal Philharmonic Society's concert, but he did not perform again in England until 1886, the year of his death.

Not in the least discouraged by the failure of his English tour, Liszt went to Germany. At this time he had befriended a young German nobleman, Prince Felix Lichnowsky, nephew of Charles Lichnowsky, one of Beethoven's patrons. The young Prince was heir to an immense fortune from large estates in East Prussia and Silesia, but because his family frowned upon his "revolutionary" ideas he had been temporarily deprived of his income and had attached himself to Liszt, from whom he had borrowed ten thousand francs.

As the two romantic young men traveled up the River Rhine, where Liszt was giving concerts to raise additional funds for the Beethoven monument, they came across the little island of Nonnenwerth. They were enchanted by the island, which was occupied by an old half-destroyed convent inhabited by only a few remaining nuns, a chapel, and some fishermen's huts. Its romantic surroundings evoked in Liszt memories of medieval German legends of the Lorelei, and the proximity of Cologne, where the largest Gothic cathedral in northern Europe was still being built, encouraged him to rent the convent for his summer home.

"I don't know why," Liszt said, "but the sight of a cathedral always moves me in a strange way. Perhaps it is because music is the architecture of sound or because architecture is crystallized music. But there is definitely a close relationship between these two arts." Liszt planned to donate his share to the completion of the Cologne cathedral.

He wrote to Marie an ecstatic letter about his discovery and asked her to join him in Nonnenwerth. But the two summers they subsequently passed in this idyllic spot did not mend matters between them. It was more for old friendship's sake and because of their children that they lived again as a family under the same roof. What Franz most probably would have liked was for Marie to lead the life of a sailor's wife, waiting patiently for him to return while he had a girl in every port. As much as she still loved Franz, Marie was not suited to such a role, and so, after two successive summers of strained reunion, she had to accept her lot. When Liszt's lease of the convent ended, so too did their eight-year-old liaison.

It would be misjudging Liszt's shrewdness to find emotional cause for their final break. He had a definite aim in his life,

Prince Felix Lichnowsky

definite plans in which neither Marie nor any other woman was included. Having tasted the fruits of fame, financial fruits in particular, he was eager to earn enough so that he could retire from public life in order to compose. And he did not love anybody enough to let her stand in his way.

Actually, Marie had at that time inherited a considerable fortune from her mother, and Liszt was earning large sums from concerts—he had recently conquered Vienna, Budapest and Germany—but neither his fame nor their finances satisfied his ambitions. He wanted more of both.

Liszt has always been considered extremely generous. But he was generous only in his later years. When a man in modest financial circumstances allows himself such noble gestures as Liszt did at the beginning of his career, it can usually be attributed to reckless extravagance. But Liszt had shrewd reasons of his own: He knew that every one of his noble gestures would repay him tenfold in publicity and eventual financial returns.

Liszt was a social climber. Neither money nor the fabulous acclaim of the public and of music critics meant as much to him as being treated on equal terms by the aristocracy. Since he was deprived of this equality by his humble origin, he was determined to gain recognition through style of living and princely behavior. The Countess d'Agoult was more of a social hindrance than a help to him.

While in Nonnenwerth, Liszt composed his *Feuilles d'Album, Die Zelle in Nonnenwerth,* and he did most of his transcriptions of the Schubert songs. He was then relearning German, which he had forgotten. Marie assisted him with the texts, as she had done at the very beginning of their relationship before they "eloped" to Geneva.

During the first summer in Nonnenwerth he wrote not a single original work of importance. He was too preoccupied with preparing his programs for the winter season, which he started by going to Berlin. This trip marked the beginning of the so-called *Glanz-Periode*—period of splendor—in his pianistic career.

While spending two months in the Prussian capital he gave as many as twenty-two concerts. An astute judge of his audiences, he substituted for his former programs of popular pieces, which merely displayed his virtuosity, a repertory of serious works from Bach to Schumann and Chopin. It goes without saying that he always also offered some of his transcriptions, except that now he dispensed with his circus rider's tricks—improvisations on given themes by the public— and even occasionally with some of his own rather tasteless works, such as *Grand Galop chromatique.*

What he did not fail to display fully was his carefully rehearsed eccentricity, both on the stage and off, for which his rich, elaborate wardrobe was as essential to him as his valet, whose prime function was to dress his hair and shave him and to give one of his three hundred and sixty cravats the appropriate appearance of aristocratic nonchalance. At his recitals he insisted that his piano should be placed not on the stage but in the middle of the hall itself and that the seats for the audience should be arranged in a circle around the instrument. Liszt was an experienced actor, well aware of the visual effect his demeanor had on an audience during a performance. While playing quiet sections in a composition he would fix his glance on someone in the hall (usually of the feminine sex) as if he were delivering some intimate message, and then, following the quickening tempo of the music, his lips would quiver and his nostrils would flare with passion until the music reached a climax and he victoriously tossed back his mane of shoulder-length hair.

Liszt's packed concerts were attended by the royal family, and the square in front of the Hôtel de Russie, where he stayed, was blackened by admirers seeking to catch a glimpse of their idol. His photographs were sold all over Berlin, and women fought bitterly over mementos such as old cigar stubs and bits of his gloves. He departed the city as if he were a hero: The royal family bade him farewell from their balcony, and Prince Lichnowsky, as his aide-de-camp, sat next to him in a coach pulled by six white horses, followed by thirty carriages, a procession of students in their colorful uniforms and a mass of admirers.

Liszt and Lichnowsky arrived in St. Petersburg, by way of Warsaw, early in the spring of 1842. Liszt felt assured of his success there because long before he had planned this tour he had gained the patronage of Empress Alexandra. He had often played for her two years earlier at Ems, where she had been taking the cure. In Weimar, in 1841, he had performed several times for Grand Duchess Maria Pavlovna, Czar Nicholas I's sister, who later in the nineteenth century played an important role in the development of Russian music. And while he was in Rome with Marie he had met Count Bielgorsky, who had arranged a concert for him at the home of Prince Gallitzin, the Governor-General of Moscow, who was wintering in Italy. Then, too, Liszt had Felix Lichnowsky, who was welcome in wealthy circles, at his side.

Count Bielgorsky took it upon himself to introduce Liszt

at his first concert in St. Petersburg at the Hall of Noblemen.
"Liszt," reported a Russian critic, "entered the hall on the arm
of Count Bielgorsky, an elderly Adonis and a typical dandy
of the forties. Bielgorsky was somewhat inclined to obesity,
moved slowly, and with prominent short-sighted eyes stared
at the brilliant assemblage. His hair was brushed back and
curled, after the manner of the Apollo Belvedere, and he wore
an enormous white cravat."

Liszt outdressed the Count. He also wore a large white
cravat, but over it shone the Order of the Golden Spur, which
he claimed to have received from Pope Pius IX. He was further adorned with various other orders dangling and clanking
from the lapels of his dress coat. But, unexpectedly, his appearance made an unfavorable impression on the Russians.
They were rather dismayed by the exhibition of his orders and
disappointed in his looks. Much had been said about his
"famous Florentine profile" and his likeness to Dante, yet
what they saw was a slender young man who stooped a great
deal, whose long hair was more appropriate to a Russian priest,
they thought, and whose face was not at all beautiful.

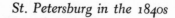

St. Petersburg in the 1840s

"There were three thousand people in the audience, Mikhail Glinka among them," the critic continued in his report. "Liszt mounted the platform, and pulling his kid gloves from his shapely white hands, tossed them carelessly on the floor. Then after acknowledging the thunderous applause, he seated himself at the piano. There was a silence as though the whole audience had been turned to stone, and Liszt, without any prelude, began the opening bars of the *William Tell Overture*. Curiosity, speculation, criticism, all were forgotten in the wonderful enchantment of his performance. His fantasia on *Don Juan*, his arrangements of Beethoven's *Adelaide* and the *Erlkönig* of Schubert, and his own *Grand Galop chromatique* followed this."

Liszt's success with the audience was indisputable, but a large segment of the Russian musical circle, to whom Glinka's opinion was sacred, was disappointed. "His drumming sounds like chopping hamburgers," said Glinka, who favored piano playing such as John Field's in his dreamlike nocturnes, and what the Russians imagined to be Chopin's. Yet on the crest of his St. Petersburg debut Liszt rode to further triumph in Moscow, where under the auspices of Prince Gallitzin he gave six concerts instead of the one originally planned.

His audiences were large, and so was the amount of money he earned and spent lavishly. Now he traveled in a coach of his own design, which could be turned into a drawing room, dining room or bedroom. Besides Lichnowsky and his valet, he traveled with a footman. The whole party was followed by admirers, some of them women dressed as boys, so the procession resembled a Gypsy king's caravan.

Liszt spent the spring of 1842 in Russia and returned for his second and last summer retreat at Nonnenwerth not only with a sizable fortune, but with memories ot a sumptuous life, which encouraged him to return to Russia during the following years.

PART III

PRINCESS WITTGENSTEIN

VIII

FROM 1841 to 1847, Franz Liszt crisscrossed the continent several times on triumphant concert tours, going as far south as Seville and Lisbon and as far east as Constantinople. While on his travels he added to his repertoire one more form of eccentricity. The manager of his tours had to provide him with a piano at the small stations, where while waiting between trains he would give a recital for a large crowd of admirers whose provincial town was too insignificant to be included on his concert itinerary.

Liszt's constant traveling kept him away from his friends, Berlioz and Chopin in particular. He corresponded with Berlioz, but his friendship with Chopin was threatened by circumstances beyond the control of both men. Liszt's life with Marie d'Agoult, barely disguised, was portrayed unflatteringly in a novel of the period, *Beatrix*, by the famous French writer Honoré de Balzac. He could only have gotten his material from George Sand. In Balzac's story, Marie is easily recognizable as the Marquise de Rochefide, who deserts her husband and family for Gennero Conti, i.e., Franz Liszt, whom the novelist describes with a sneer as both composer and singer "of Neapolitan origin, but born in Marseille."

It took all of Franz's *sang froid* to calm Marie. She sug-

Marie d'Agoult

gested indignantly that he should challenge Balzac. Franz wisely advised her to disregard any resemblances between Balzac's characters and the two of them.

But this was not the only time that Chopin, as a friend of Sand's, and Liszt, as a friend of Marie's, found themselves in a rather awkward situation. Almost at the same time as Balzac's book appeared, Sand published her own *Horace,* an even worse indictment of Marie. Sand portrayed her Marie-modeled character, Madame de Chailly, as a woman "terrifyingly slim, who had doubtful teeth and dry skin, was arrogant and overloaded with rings, and had a purchased title —in short, her nobility was as artificial as everything else about her—teeth, bosom, and heart."

Marie was incensed, and in her letters to Franz she reproached both Sand and Chopin bitterly. Liszt, far away on his tours, could only take Marie's side and sympathize with her. Two years later, on February 6, 1843, he wrote to Chopin from Posen, in Poland:

. . . I am especially anxious to send greetings and to seize this occasion to repeat again, at the risk of appearing monotonous, that my affection and admiration for you will always be the same, and that you can always make use of me in any way whatever.

But the friendship of the two men had suffered in the embroilment of two bitter women. Chopin did not answer Liszt's letter, and they never saw each other again.

Perhaps if Franz had been living once more in Paris, where he could have seen Chopin as in the old days, the break between them would not have been permanent, but Liszt's concert tours and interests were taking him farther and farther away from France.

After his first trip to Russia, he went to Weimar for the marriage of Grand Duchess Maria Pavlovna's son. The Grand Duchess, to whom Liszt partially owed his glamorous introduction in Russia, suggested that he spend a few months a year in Weimar as conductor and musical director to the grand ducal court of Charles Augustus, a well-known patron of the arts.

This suggestion suited Franz, for despite his large earnings from concerts, an assured regular salary was exactly what he had been wanting for some time. According to the terms of his contract, Liszt could not only devote a good part of each year to touring, but could, with the support of the court, use the concert hall or opera house to produce any work of his choice.

He began his duties in Weimar in 1844, but in August of the following year, before returning to the town, he attended the Beethoven Festival organized in connection with the unveiling of the Beethoven monument in Bonn.

The occasion turned out to be a bitter disappointment for him. His stipulation that Bartolini cast the monument had been waived in favor of a bronze bust by a German sculptor. The accommodations for the thousands of visitors, including the royal families of England and Prussia and many eminent musicians, were inadequate, and the concert hall, to seat three thousand, had not been completed because of lack of funds.

He was not treated as he had been in Russia, where no criticism was voiced either against his humble origin or his private life. The Bonn burghers thought Liszt an upstart, a vagabond, who was making a fool of himself all over Europe, and they implied that his donation to the monument had prevented their own sponsors from appearing on the same list of contributors. Still, they had to accept his additional financial help or the building of the hall would never have been completed.

At the opening of the festival, Liszt conducted Beethoven's *Symphony in C minor* and the last scene from *Fidelio* and played the *Emperor Concerto*. Two days later, at the close of the three-day festival, he presented his own cantata, especially written for the occasion, in which he surpassed what had been expected of him as a composer. But at the banquet that followed, where everyone at all connected with the event was given a toast, Liszt was not mentioned. And when he raised his glass to the nations that honored Beethoven, he made the fatal mistake of forgetting to name France. The omission caused protestations and loud disputes, ending in a general uproar, with women leaving the hall, while Liszt protested in vain his indebtedness to the slighted country.

The newspapers blamed him for everything and accused his generosity of being merely another scheme for personal publicity: "Beethoven Festival in Honor of Franz Liszt" was one of the many sarcastic headlines.

Always prone to collapse when facing adverse criticism, Liszt now suffered from a gall-bladder attack and went to Baden-Baden for the cure. Like so many far less capable men, he was struck suddenly with the idea that marriage might solve all his problems. He wanted the comfort of a wife, and with this in mind he courted a niece of Alphonse Lamartine, the French poet. She was young, pretty, and had money and a title—her name was Valerie Countess Cassiat. Lamartine knew Liszt very well, however, and would not recommend him as a husband. Liszt proposed marriage only once in his life, and Valerie was the only woman who said no to him.

But this setback did not change his mind. The time had come for him to find a way to stop giving concerts and to devote himself entirely to composing. He needed two things: money and feminine company. It is a mistaken idea that only businessmen and kingdoms require money and that all an artist needs is a piece of paper and a pencil or a pen. Liszt was not a man to live in a garret. Rightly or not, he felt he was a patrician, and neither his growing impatience with the life and profession of a performer nor the urge for composing that he felt ever stronger as time passed would drive him to accepting what in his opinion was a mediocre existence. And he needed a woman with whom he could share not only his triumphs, but on whose moral support he could depend when he was depressed by self-doubt.

If Liszt could complain against fate for not having been

born of a noble family, he could never complain of being un-
lucky. As a youngster he was fortunate enough to have
wealthy Hungarians sponsor his musical education and to
have Czerny teach him how to practice piano and give him
the foundation of a technique. As a young man he was fortunate enough to have the Countess d'Agoult love him,
teach him the elementary manners of the society whose acceptance he craved and guide him in his work.

In 1847, Liszt went once again to Russia. He arrived in
Kiev during the first days of February for a series of concerts.
At one of these he was heard by a young woman who already
knew his *Paternoster*, which had been performed in a local
Catholic church. Upon her return home she sent a hundred
rubles to the benefit performance Liszt was to give. He felt
compelled to call on her and thank her for her generous
donation.

Franz was superstitious, as most artists are, so he was
startled when he learned that the young woman's name was
Carolyne—the same as his first love, whom only two years
before (she was then the Countess d'Artigau) he had seen
again and for the last time at a concert while on his way
from a tour in Spain.

There was little similarity between the two women, except
that, as Liszt soon learned, both were devout Catholics.

Carolyne was blond, with a pale complexion and clear
blue eyes. Her plump figure was invariably dressed in a simple
black robe with a loose jacket, and she always wore a black
lace cap with lilac ribbons that she tied under her chin. She
was fond of smoking strong cigars, a habit she had developed
during her long reading sessions with her father, but in no
other way could she have been compared to George Sand or
the beautiful Marie d'Agoult. Carolyne's fashion-loving
mother had to find consolation in the thought that her
daughter would be prettier after the Resurrection. Extremely

*The Princess Carolyne Sayn-Wittgenstein
(here painted as a brunette) with her daughter, Maria*

sensitive to a woman's appearance, Liszt was attracted by
what he called Carolyne's "spiritual beauty"—but her charm
was no doubt enhanced by her immense fortune of three
million rubles (comparable to about ten million dollars today, her royal title and her religious devotion, which in
himself he had almost forgotten because it was irrelevant to
his worldly career.

Fourteen years had passed since Liszt had first known
Marie d'Agoult. He was no longer a penniless musician strug-

gling for recognition, but a world-famous virtuoso. Carolyne was determined, as Marie had been, to help him devote his time to composing, but the circumstances were more favorable now than they had been a decade before.

Princess Jeanne Elisabeth Carolyne von Sayn-Wittgenstein was the daughter of Peter Iwanowski and Pauline Podowska. Her parents were Poles, but her father owned property in Russia, where Carolyne was born and brought up. By coincidence, her story partially resembled that of Marie d'Agoult. At seventeen she, too, married a man she did not love, and with the same results. She had one daughter, Princess Maria, born the year after the marriage. Her husband, Prince Nicolas von Sayn-Wittgenstein—of a Russian branch of the Westphalian family and an aide-de-camp to the Czar —was a cavalry officer who did not share his young bride's intellectual interests, which she acquired from her father while her mother was away on pleasure trips in Europe.

When Liszt and Carolyne met she was twenty-eight— Marie d'Agoult's age when *she* had fallen in love. Like Marie, estranged from her husband though not formally divorced, Carolyne would have "eloped" with Liszt had practicalities not prevented her from traveling with him to Weimar.

After their first meeting, the Princess invited Liszt to Woronince in Padolia, one of her principal estates. With its oak woods, lakes, parks, flower gardens, and wide tree-lined avenues so long that they seemed endless, Woronince was as large as one of the provinces in Germany or France.

As was to be expected, the furnishings in the great mansion created a specific atmosphere in each of the enormous, ornately roofed rooms. Gray and red dominated Carolyne's boudoir, complete with oriental rugs and divans and a crucifix that rose to the ceiling. In the library, which was blue, works of Goethe and Dante lay open on a long refectory table. The music room, in addition to its many sofas, had a large bearskin on the floor reserved for the mistress of the house to lounge on while listening to music and smoking a cigar. The whole establishment was attended by a vast number of servants, who dispensed their duties silently or, when ordered, entertained the guests with singing and dancing.

Even Liszt, who had seen many other magnificent estates, was dazzled by the splendor. He remained there for several weeks, and after completing his concert engagements he returned for a prolonged stay of four months. In October he gave a recital in Elizabetgrad, a small provincial town south of Kiev, which he had announced was going to be the last concert of his pianistic career. "Since then," Liszt said some time later, "I have not earned a single penny by piano playing, teaching, or conducting. All this . . . only cost me time and money."

He did not bother to mark this important event in his career with a farewell celebration. He was anxious to return to the Princess, with whom he had already laid plans that would solve all his financial problems in the future. He was to go back to Weimar, and she was to join him there as soon as she had arranged for the administration of her estates, transferred part of her fortune abroad, and made personal arrangements for her departure.

At that time is was necessary for every Russian subject to obtain special government authorization for traveling outside the country. Obstacles of one kind or another were always encountered. Only because of the Princess' connections was she granted a permit to go to Carlsbad, a health resort in Bohemia. Rumors about her amorous scheme had already reached the ears of those in high government circles. Then her departure was almost thwarted by the Czar's order forbidding all travel in or out of Russia because of the revolution of 1848, which started in France and spread through most of the Central European countries. But the Princess and her

The revolution of 1848 in Dresden, Germany

daughter, accompanied by carriages packed with as many personal belongings as could be taken without arousing undue suspicion, passed the frontier shortly before the toll gate came down.

During the months of their separation, Carolyne's constant correspondence with Liszt was filled with either radiant hope of an imminent meeting or utter despair because of the difficulties of leaving Russia. What Carolyne was completely unaware of was that Liszt did not take his escapade seriously, that he had spoken the vows of love as lightly as he had on many similar occasions. He found it difficult to reply in kind to Carolyne's passionate letters, for no sooner had he returned to Weimar than he was living in his hotel with another woman.

Only because the court and the people of Weimar were anxious to have Liszt continue his musical activities there did they close their eyes to his conduct. But he was horror-stricken to receive a letter from Carolyne announcing her decision to "make the sacrifice" and asking that he meet her at the Austrian border. Suspecting that "sacrifice" meant the abandoning of her fortune, he tried, as eloquently as he could, to persuade her to remain in Russia and terminate their relationship.

But the Princess was on her way, and he had to at least appear chivalrous. This time Prince Lichnowsky came to his assistance. He sent one of his men to escort Carolyne and her daughter to his castle, Krzynawoitz, which he lent to Liszt for his *tête-à-tête* with Carolyne—he himself was going to be absent in Berlin.

At first Liszt could not even feign affection for Carolyne, but when he learned that she had retained a part of her "extra charm," that out of her fortune she had managed to transfer abroad at least two million roubles, his appreciation of her "sacrifice" increased. With only a few servants in the castle, they enjoyed an idyllic Eden, similar to that of Carolyne's own home, for the blossoming of their love.

There is no doubt that with time Liszt became not merely attached to Carolyne, but entirely dependent on her, and that, in his own fashion, he loved her more than any other woman in his life. At the castle they read together once again, as they had done at Woronince, but without the intellectual uneasiness that had often disturbed Franz's relationship with Countess d'Agoult. They discussed further their plans for "uniting the arts," an idea that appealed to Carolyne, who was better versed in literature and the visual arts than she was in music. And there were hours when Liszt did not merely talk about his future compositions, but actually worked at them.

He completed the *Glanes de Woronince*, three transcriptions of Polish melodies, which were inspired by songs he had heard on Carolyne's estate, and he sketched his second symphonic poem, *Hungaria*, though he did not finish the composition. His mind was on a different subject.

"Ineffable secrets are revealed to me through you and for you," said Liszt to Carolyne. "Henceforth I shall be able to die in peace blessing your name. . . . All my hope, all my faith, all my love are concentrated and summed up in you— *et nunc et semper*. May the Lord's angel lead you, oh you who are my radiant morning star."

Carolyne, for the first time in love, reciprocated with even more flowery testimonies of her passion.

In conversations far into the night, and during their long walks in the park of Krzynawoitz, Carolyne made her lover reveal everything about his life before they met. She was quite prepared to follow him to his artistic heights, but was dismayed by his humble origin, which Liszt always seemed unable to disguise. He puzzled Carolyne with his grotesque reverence for titles—even in such a small matter as addressing her with the formal and respectful *Sie* rather than the more familiar *Du*. Discreetly flattering him by her desire to "know everything about him," she insisted that he take her through Raiding and Eisenstadt before going to Weimar.

The Princess never revealed her impressions of the house

and environment in which Franz had spent his boyhood, yet the similarities between the background of the steward's son and that of any caretaker on her own estate in Russia could not have escaped her. Apparently Carolyne was as much in love with Liszt as Marie had been, and she preferred to ignore anything that could have unsettled her mind or heart. In July 1848, they arrived in Weimar, where she was to begin a life of her own choice.

IX

*W*EIMAR, once the home of Goethe and Schiller, was a small town of twelve thousand inhabitants. There was the court, at which Liszt and Carolyne had Grand Duchess Maria Pavlovna as a friend, and there were the typical provincial burghers, about whose attitude the lovers had to be most careful.

In the beginning, Carolyne and Liszt lived separately. He rented an apartment at the Hotel Erbprinz, while she took quarters in the Altenburg, a roomy house on a little hill outside the town. There, in an annex, Carolyne set apart two rooms for Liszt: a bedroom and a studio with a low ceiling and a view of the garden. The studio contained only a few pieces of furniture—his desk, a piano and a few chairs—and only two pictures on the walls: Durer's engraving of *Melancholia* and a drawing of *St. François de Paule marchant sur les flots,* which inspired Liszt's well-known composition by the same name, though it did not appear in its final form until some sixteen years later.

The two rooms were austere in comparison to the luxurious apartment occupied by Carolyne and her daughter. Besides the bedrooms there were four large drawing rooms. Liszt's concert grand piano was in the largest, and an assortment of his trophies and mementos were in the others—the famous

jeweled saber presented to him by his countrymen dominat-
ing a number of other swords, Turkish coffee trays, oriental
tables inlaid with mother-of-pearl and a row of pipes.

Later the Grand Duchess bought the Altenburg, and Carolyne was then able to rent the whole house from her so that
Liszt's own music room and library could be on the second
floor with his favorite Erard concert grand, a large collection
of music scores and manuscripts, and the small piano on
which Mozart is supposed to have played.

While Carolyne was still hoping to obtain a divorce from
her husband, Liszt continued for appearance's sake to live
at the hotel in town. Ever since her flight from Russia in
March 1848, Carolyne had protested that she had been a
minor and unwilling to marry her husband in the first place,
but neither Prince Wittgenstein nor his family were willing
to part with her large fortune, and even the Grand Duchess'
personal plea to her brother the Czar failed to turn the
monarch's favor against the Prince, his aide-de-camp.

The divorce was barred and Carolyne's estates were con-
fiscated. After she refused to return home, Carolyne was
formally banished from Russia. For political reasons she was
no longer received at the Weimar court, and some of the
courtiers refrained from associating with her too openly.

Since there was no longer any reason for Liszt to remain
at his hotel, he moved to the Altenburg—though all official
documents during the following years of his stay in Weimar
were addressed to him at the Hotel Erbprinz.

It was from the Altenburg that Liszt directed the musical
affairs of the town, which influenced musical life everywhere
else; and it was in the Altenburg that he composed most of
his major works. During the following ten years his energy
and creative ability did more for music and musicians than
anyone else's in the same length of time.

As a self-appointed patron of music, he studied the manu-

Richard Wagner, 1813–1883

scripts sent to him by aspiring young composers, recommended the promising ones to publishers and undertook to give many works their first performances. He wrote pamphlets and articles on musical aesthetics as well as critical works on *Fidelio*, Gluck's *Orfeo ed Euridice*, and the early operas of Wagner. He spent much time and energy on launching a Goethe Foundation, which was to sponsor annual international contests for musicians, painters and poets. This project, however, was abandoned for lack of participants.

During his first spring in Weimar, during the second week of May, Liszt was surprised by a visit from Richard Wagner, who after the abortive 1849 revolution in Dresden had come as a political fugitive to find refuge in Weimar. Liszt knew Wagner as the composer of the operas *Rienzi* and *Tannhäuser*, but of Wagner the man he knew practically nothing at all.

The two had met for the first time in Paris in 1840, when Liszt was enjoying his success and reputation as the world's greatest pianist, while Wagner, two years younger than he, was still a poor struggling composer who, having failed in Germany, had come to Paris to seek his fortune. Unprepossessing in appearance—he was of medium height and looked undernourished—Wagner betrayed his Saxon middle-class background by the way he dressed, his provincial manners and the strong accent in his speech. He inspired no romantic attachments in Parisian society—he did not even play any instrument that could have introduced him into the circles that had welcomed Chopin and Liszt. Liszt barely took notice of him, and Wagner, who had never been impressed by anyone except himself, in turn resented Liszt's success in the world from which he was excluded.

Almost exactly a year later, in April 1841, Wagner called on Liszt at home, with only one object in mind—to borrow some money. But Wagner found Liszt in a company where everyone spoke French, and since he had no command of the language he could not join in the conversation. Having failed to gain Liszt's attention in discussing Schubert with him, he left the reception without mentioning the object of his visit.

A few days later, however, he received from Liszt's secretary a complimentary ticket to Liszt's forthcoming concerts. While Wagner could not conceal his wonder at Liszt's performances, his aversion to the behavior of the audiences led him to send to the Dresden *Abendzeitung* scorching reviews of the concerts, at which, he remarked, Liszt charged twenty francs admission for mere piano playing and cleared ten thousand francs profit. Since Liszt was "amassing a fortune by piano strumming" while *he*, the German idealist, was starving, Wagner saw no possible spiritual kinship with him,

a man who was not even a conductor and was therefore
of no use to him.

But after Liszt had captured the Russian millionairess and
had begun his activities in Weimar, Wagner's attitude toward him changed perceptibly. He lost no time in writing to
Liszt:

. . . Things have been going badly with me, and it suddenly
occurs to me that you might help me. I have undertaken upon
myself the publication of my three operas. The sum in question
amounts to five thousand thalers [a thaler was worth about a
dollar]. Could you get it for me? Have you got it, or has someone
got it who would give it for love of you?

The clumsy insinuation about Carolyne did not escape
Liszt, but the letter writer added another typical Wagnerian
touch that he apparently believed could not fail to win
Liszt's favor:

Would it not be most interesting for you to become the publisher-
proprietor of my operas? And do you realize what would come of
it? I should become a *man*, a man to whom existence would be
possible, an artist who would never need to ask for another penny
in his life, who would be content to work with enthusiasm and
pleasure. My dear Liszt, with this money you could buy me out
of servitude. Do you think that as a serf I am worth that price?

Liszt had his own plans for the use of Carolyne's money,
and they did not include sharing it with anyone. He did not
go himself to hear Wagner's *Tannhäuser* in Dresden, but
sent Carolyne as his ambassador. She was so enthusiastic
about the opera that she brought the score back to Liszt, who
at the first opportunity introduced *Tannhäuser* in Weimar.
Wagner could not attend the Weimar performance because at
that time he was dabbling in revolutionary activities in
Dresden.

No musician would have been blamed for aspiring to better

social conditions, but Wagner aroused the authorities' suspicion when he stepped out of the sphere of art into that of politics. He wrote inflammatory articles and took part in clandestine meetings of men plotting an uprising in Dresden, and he was the one who wrote to Prague for a supply of hand grenades and weapons. During the five days of actual fighting in the streets of the city he ran errands for the revolutionaries, since he could not carry a musket or be of any use at the barricades, and served as an observer from the belfry of a church.

It is true that whenever his comrades seemed to be losing ground, Wagner was the first to leave, but he was also the first to return as soon as their position improved. Although he denied the charges brought against him by the government, he was nonetheless aware that he could be arrested at any time in Weimar, and with Liszt's help he escaped first to Zurich and then to Paris.

During Wagner's brief visit in Weimar, Liszt had realized that, despite his unscrupulousness and his incredible egotism, Wagner was an idealist about his art. Liszt's personal feelings never stood in the way where art was concerned. He did not see Wagner during the following four years, but he constantly assisted him not only financially, but with his advice and through his connections in Paris, London and Vienna—in fact everywhere where his influence could be helpful.

On August 28, 1850, Liszt produced *Lohengrin* in Weimar, and it was due to him that Wagner was commissioned to write *Siegfried's Death*, the nucleus of *Der Ring des Nibelungen*. Wagner's other grandiloquent ideas might never have been realized were it not for Liszt's suggestions, encouragement and influence—and we would have been deprived of *Der Ring*, or *Tristan und Isolde*, or *Die Meistersinger von Nürnberg*, or *Parsifal*.

A few months later, after Wagner's escape abroad, Liszt

tried again to show that, as far as he was concerned, the art of a man stood above his own personal relationship with the artist. Chagrined by the death of Frederic Chopin in 1849, and in spite of the ultimate coldness between them, Liszt felt compelled to write a book in tribute to the composer. He soon discovered, however, that for an authoritative book he had rather scant personal knowledge of Chopin, and he wrote to Chopin's sister, Ludwika Jedrzejevicz, for information. He sent her twelve questions concerning Chopin's background, his family, his education, his political views, the details of his relationship with George Sand, their trip to Majorca, and his illness. As might have been expected only one month after her brother's death, Ludwika was in no mood to review Chopin's intimate life for Liszt, and her answers, though perfectly cordial, were more evasive than illuminating.

Nevertheless, a book on Chopin eventually appeared in print—a book to which Liszt should never have signed his name. If it was not written entirely by Carolyne, it certainly had the mark of her close collaboration, which in fact she coyly admitted: "When two beings have so completely merged, can it ever be said where the work of one begins or the other ends?"

Collaboration had been a different matter in the past, when Liszt gave Marie d'Agoult the general idea and a few specific suggestions for an article and left the actual writing of the piece to her. Marie had perfect command of the French language and an acceptable style, while Carolyne lacked both. In addition, the book deals not with Chopin the man, as originally intended, but principally with irrelevant matters—mazurkas and polonaises in general, the glories of the aristocratic spirit, ramblings about Polish nobility and events in the history of Poland. If substantially shortened, this material could have had a place in an exhaustive study of Chopin, but not in a book of one hundred and eighty-five pages.

Carolyne's claim to a talent for writing rested on her twenty-eight volumes on religious subjects, to which she devoted the rest of her life. Years later, her writings were criticized as a "literary Tower of Babel . . . German written in

A scene from an early performance of Wagner's Tannhäuser

French . . . a translation, indeed, by a Pole who did not understand the original."

Liszt himself, not sure about her style or the correct form for a book on Chopin, sent the manuscript to the writer Sainte-Beuve, asking for his assistance. Sainte-Beuve replied:

Dear friend, you cannot doubt that I would have done the little revision you requested with alacrity if it had been physically possible. . . . Glancing over your interesting and generous appreciation, it would be necessary, it seems to me, in order to cast it into French as I understand it, to begin again and rewrite the entire work, and I am in no position at the moment to undertake this.

However, the book was published in France. A revised edition worse than the first followed, and the book was translated into German and was even published in the United States in 1963. It can merely serve as an additional testimony to Liszt's blind faith in Carolyne's intellectual resources and his love for her.

Liszt kept the mornings for his own compositions, and in the Altenburg, with Carolyne at his elbow, so to speak, he wrote some of his immortal works. Despite his preoccupation with piano literature during the years devoted to giving concerts, or perhaps because of his new activities as conductor of the symphonic and opera repertory in Weimar, he succeeded in developing a certain technique for writing orchestral works. During this period he composed the *Twelve Symphonic Poems*, one of which—*Héroide Funèbre*—was a revision of his *Revolutionary Symphony*, which dated back to 1830, when he was an enthusiastic disciple of Saint-Simon. Liszt's revolutionary sympathies had been somewhat shaken by the death of Prince Felix Lichnowsky, who had been killed in a street fight in Dresden during the revolution of 1848.

He dedicated the whole collection of *Symphonic Poems*, a form of composition he originated, to Carolyne:

To her who has fulfilled her faith through love—whose hope has grown greater in the midst of sorrow—who has built her happiness upon sacrifice. To her who remains the companion of my life, the firmament of my mind, the living prayer and the Heaven of my soul—to Jeanne Elisabeth Carolyne.

This flamboyant inscription clearly expresses Liszt's and Carolyne's devotion to each other. Even the slightest separation—perhaps a concert he had to conduct out of town or a cure she was taking—seemed to them a calamity that they could ease only by constant passionate correspondence. The occasional visitor was an intruder in their idyll, and they actually managed to pass short notes to each other behind their unsuspecting guest's back.

As jealous and possessive as Carolyne was, she did not let her feelings interfere with Liszt's compositions inspired by "another woman." He now began to work on his *Faust Symphony*, of which he had spoken to Marie d'Agoult after their daily readings of Goethe during their happy days at Lake Como.

Liszt carried Goethe's work on his travels, and the more he penetrated the philosophical aspects of it, the more he felt akin to it. He saw himself endowed with all the resources of an extraordinary talent, yet he felt the supreme gift of creation had been denied him. His cherished desire was to write operas, but his one and only attempt in his youth had failed, and now at last, when he had acquired sufficient experience and could devote himself to this form of composition, he was confronted by Richard Wagner's creations, which already embodied his own ideas of a new opera and revealed a mastery of writing he did not believe he could surpass.

He did not complete his *Faust Symphony* until 1861, but in 1856 he finished the *Dante Symphony*, which also had taken many years of contemplation and work. This piece owed its birth in his mind to Marie d'Agoult's readings of the

Divine Comedy. Because he did not feel equal to the task at that time, Liszt merely daydreamed of a large orchestral work on Dante's theme, and his impressions were expressed on a smaller scale in his *Fantaisie quasi sonata, d'Après une lecture de Dante.* But later he planned the symphony in appropriately grandiose style, dividing it into three major parts—*Inferno, Purgatorio* and *Paradiso*—and closing the composition with an elaborate *Magnificat* with chorus.

Liszt kept up an extensive correspondence with friends, composers and admirers, and before long he was besieged by young pianists who wanted to study under him or at least ask his advice. This period marked the beginning of Liszt's "piano school," from which came a whole procession of illustrious performers who passed on to the generation after them the technique of playing that they had studied with the master.

It is a matter of conjecture whether this association with the aspiring concert pianists of the day led Liszt once again to write for the piano. In 1849, in addition to his *Etudes Transcendantes,* which he kept revising, he wrote the three *Etudes de concert* (in A flat, F minor and D flat), as well as another set of two *Etudes de concert: Das Waldesrauschen*

Two contemporary caricatures of Liszt (left) and Wagner (right)

and *Die Gnomenreigen*. And in 1854, after finishing the two *Ballades* (in A and B minor), he finally wrote his *Sonata in B minor*. Most of his piano works remain in the repertory of concert pianists today, but the *Sonata in B minor*, though its content is rather dated, stands apart as a supreme test of their technical skill.

While in Weimar, Liszt also wrote his *Hungarian Rhapsodies*, which became so popular that even as late as the beginning of this century no piano recital was considered complete without one of them at the end of the program. He had become acquainted with Hungarian Gypsy music in his childhood, and he heard it again whenever he returned to Hungary. Liszt was not the only composer to use Hungarian melodies, but he was the one who coined the term "rhapsody" to signify the character of such pieces and the freedom of interpretation they required—a freedom from scholastic rules, born of the natural musicianship of Gypsies, which fascinated Liszt. Unfortunately, the *Hungarian Rhapsodies* have become hackneyed for today's audiences, probably because they were used so often by pianists as showpieces of virtuosity. When they are no longer studied pedantically but performed à la Gypsy, perhaps their charm will be revived.

It is regrettable that most students and even concert pianists, while spending hours, weeks and months mastering his compositions, seldom take time to acquaint themselves with the literary works and poems that inspired certain compositions—*Petrarch Sonnets, Liebestraum, Mephisto Waltz* and *Mazeppa*, to mention a few. Such reading could not fail to improve their conceptions of these pieces and bring their performances closer to the composer's intentions.

As a teacher, Liszt seldom gratified his pupils by playing through an entire composition. The author was told by Moritz Rosenthal and Émile Sauer, who were illustrious representatives of his school, that Liszt mostly talked about the composition in question, and that while illustrating certain sections he played everything *mezzo forte*. Even in dramatic moments requiring *forte* he merely made the appropriate gestures without increasing his volume. Apparently he followed the maxim that a loud sound can be heard anyway, but you have to *listen* to a soft-spoken word.

Although generous with the time he gave to teaching, Liszt's main interest was making Weimar the center of music in Europe. For his great plans, however, the town had rather limited resources. To begin with, it took all Liszt's energy to bring the provincial orchestra up to the desired standard of a well-trained ensemble such as we enjoy today. Having known only "time-beating" conductors, the men of the Weimar orchestra complained when Liszt dispensed with a baton and merely indicated with his hands the phrasing and dynamics of the composition, often leaving the musicians on their own during a whole section.

He was finally forced to compromise. He agreed to use the jewel-studded baton Carolyne had given him, although he still refused to just beat time. And with infinite patience he succeeded not only in making first-rate performers out of the provincial musicians, but by dwelling on every detail during rehearsals he introduced to them the brilliant virtuoso qualities of execution so typical of conductors who have been concert pianists.

Liszt produced a staggering list of meticulously rehearsed operas: Gluck's *Orfeo ed Euridice, Iphigénie en Tauride, Armide,* and *Alceste;* Mozart's *Don Giovanni* and *The Magic Flute;* Beethoven's *Fidelio,* then still unfamiliar to the public; Jacques Halévy's *La Juive,* and several operas by Cherubini and Spontini. His major achievement in this field, however, was the introduction of Wagner's operas, which led to a renewed close friendship between the two composers. But at the end of some years of undeniable accomplishment, Liszt had to acknowledge the failure of his plan to make Weimar the musical center of the world.

He was disappointed that his idea—a great one in his opinion—of rejuvenating music by allying it more intimately with the other arts had fallen on barren ground. Liszt in his own works was always stimulated by literature, poetry and the visual arts, and it was his dream to use the wealth of these sources as the basis for all musical composition. It is true that if he had wished, upon his arrival in Weimar in 1848, to enslave himself to the music of the past, to the good and healthy traditions that had glorified music from the time of Palestrina to Mendelssohn, he could have done it, and probably he would have been more popular with the Weimar audiences. But his convictions were too sincere, his faith in the art of his time and the future too ardent; he was not impressed by the idle cries of the pseudo-classicists that contemporary art was losing its meaning. But because of the deaths of the Grand Duchess and Grand Duke Charles Augustus, the two staunchest supporters of his projects, Liszt's opportunity was lost in Weimar. The young Grand Duke,

Charles Alexander, favored theatrical performances rather than music.

It was Liszt's ambition to create a foundation, a root, for Wagner's masterpieces on German soil, but their composer was in exile, and all the opera houses in Germany were afraid to have his name on their programs. Liszt could not convince the Grand Duke to produce Wagner's *Der Ring des Nibelungen* in Weimar, and so he knew that he and his hopes were at a dead end.

His liaison with Carolyne was certainly no help. The Grand Duke was influenced by the scandalized attitude of the burghers and their wives. "If I stayed so long in Weimar," Liszt said, "it was only because I was sustained by a spirit that was not lacking in nobility—the honor, the dignity, the fine character of a woman against infamous persecutions."

He failed to see, however, that Carolyne's behavior antagonized the townspeople. They resented not only her "dubious morals," but her obvious contempt for them and her habit of smoking in public—behavior not tolerated in the Germany of that time. Carolyne neither sought nor had any friends in Weimar, and the few people who were well disposed toward her reported that she was lacking in feminine charm and was tactless and much too dogmatic in her opinions.

And, whether because of Carolyne or not, Liszt himself lacked support for his plans. He was polite to those at the court, but he did nothing to ingratiate himself with the burghers, whom he called jackasses. He invariably spoke French—which he knew better than German, a language he misused with a strong Hungarian accent—and his weird theatrical appearance made him seem an intruder. Besides, he seemed to have completely overlooked the fact that these "jackasses" could not afford to finance his grand projects and were satisfied with theatrical productions that required neither his nor Carolyne's presence and were much less costly.

Liszt was restless. There were several personal reasons for this. During their stay in Weimar, Carolyne had not only taken complete charge of his daily life, but had insisted that he should do something about Blandine and Cosima, who— in her opinion—were leading useless lives in Paris because the Countess d'Agoult could not "manage" to have time for them. As a first step, she suggested that Liszt ask them to come to the Altenburg. She discreetly departed for a short stay in Paris before the girls' arrival in August 1855.

Blandine, nineteen, and Cosima, two years younger, com-

Goethe's house in Weimar

pletely upset their father's daily schedule. He was used to going to bed early and arising not later than six in the morning to begin his work, but now the girls kept him up past midnight with their innumerable stories. And, chattering gaily, they joined him for breakfast, a time when even Carolyne knew it was better to leave him alone.

After several weeks of this reunion, Liszt grew fond of the young ladies, though he was glad to see Hans von Bülow's mother come to fetch them to Berlin, where she kept a boarding house. To von Bülow, one of his most talented disciples as both pianist and conductor, Liszt had entrusted his daughters' musical education. Two years later, on August 18, 1857, Cosima married Hans, in the presence of her delighted father. Blandine returned to France, where, on her father's birthday, October 22, she married Émile Olliver, the French statesman and minister of Napoleon III. Thus both daughters were once again out of Liszt's and Carolyne's life.

His son Daniel, who had been studying law in Vienna, went to visit Cosima in Berlin, but the twenty-year-old boy suffered from tuberculosis, and he died there. This blow was soon followed by another. Carolyne's daughter Maria, whom Liszt nicknamed Magnolette and whom he was fonder of than his own children, married Prince Constantine Hohenlohe and went to live with her husband in Vienna, leaving the Altenburg deserted, since Carolyne had already departed for Rome to plead her divorce case against her husband before a church court.

It took only a minor incident to precipitate the final crisis in Liszt's relationship with the court and the people of Weimar. On December 18, 1858, he conducted *Der Barbier von Bagdad*, an opera by one of his pupils, Peter Cornelius. Liszt was hissed for the performance, and upon his return home that night, he sent a letter to the Grand Duke resigning his post at the Weimar court.

X

*A*T EVERY crisis in his life, Liszt turned to religion or sought solace in feminine company. Carolyne's daily letters from Rome were not sufficient to direct his rudderless existence. And soon he was no longer as busy with his work as he was with making love to his pretty pupils. One of them seemed to have gained his special favor, for after 1855, when she had completed her two-year course of study with him, she remained his confidante.

Liszt corresponded with her until the end of his life. His letters to her were posthumously published in a separate volume in the four-volume collection of his correspondence. It appeared under the title of *Briefe zu einer Freundin*, or "Letters to Madame X," so the girl's name was kept a secret.

She was German, presumably from Hanover. According to those who had no reason to be biased, she had a nice disposition, "little character of her own, and in certain matters was not always sincere." But she was an attractive young woman in her twenties, and Liszt considered her beautiful.

Agnes Denis-Street's maiden name was Klindworth. No one knew much about her husband, who might have been dead or separated from her by this time, except that he was supposed to have fathered her two little boys, with whom she arrived in Weimar in 1853. She led a quiet life in her apart-

ment near the theater in Karlsplatz and would not even have
been noticed by the townspeople had it not been for her
Parisian dresses and the fact that Liszt often directed his
afternoon walks from the Altenburg to her lodgings, where
upon his arrival the windows were closed and the curtains
prudently drawn. Avid for further information, the townspeople had to be content with reports whispered by the servants at the Altenburg that Agnes' name was frequently mentioned in excited arguments between Liszt and their mistress,
Princess Carolyne.

The reason for the mystery about Liszt's relationship with
Agnes is that musicologists and biographers of musicians
treat their subjects as if they lived in a sort of musical vacuum,
and thus they often miss certain valuable information that
can be obtained through research in an entirely different field.

There would have been no data available about Agnes'
two-year sojourn in Weimar and her close friendship with
Liszt if, after he left the town, he had not taken one of his
short vacations from Carolyne and accompanied Agnes to
Düsseldorf. At a concert there he introduced her to Hans
von Bülow's old friend Ferdinand Lassalle, the famous German socialist whose name in the history of Germany stands
next to Karl Marx on one side and the monarchist Bismarck
on the other. A study of Lassalle's personal life reveals facts
of which Liszt remained completely ignorant.

Agnes was not a pianist of the caliber that Liszt usually
accepted as a pupil, and whether it was at Agnes' request or
his suggestion, her "private" lessons took place at her apartment and not at the Altenburg, where his pupils had their
lessons as a class. Socially, however, Agnes was a frequent,
discreetly eager visitor to the Altenburg. But neither Liszt
nor the usually astute Carolyne ever suspected that Agnes
was only an instrument in an intrigue involving her father,
for they knew nothing about her true background.

Hans von Bülow,
1830–1894
(Painting by
Lenbach)

Agnes' father, George Klindworth, then in his fifties, was considered by those who were well informed to be one of the most disreputable scoundrels of his time. A former school-teacher, actor, theatrical manager and shady journalist, he made a good if precarious living as a spy and informer for several countries simultaneously.

He had been employed as a secret intelligence agent, at one time or other, by Guizot, then the Prime Minister of France; Manteuffel, the Prussian general; Louis Napoleon; and Nicholas I of Russia. He had a guaranteed income of one thousand francs a month, free quarters and free travel, and in addition made another thousand thalers each month from side jobs. Klindworth used his young daughter Agnes as an agent of his own. He kept an apartment for her in Brussels, though she usually traveled with him.

Agnes came to Weimar on a twofold assignment her father
had received from the Russian authorities: She was to spy
on Carolyne and Liszt, and even more important to make
Liszt fall in love with her and lure him away from the Princess. Carolyne was almost twenty years older than Agnes, and
Liszt's susceptibility to pretty young women was fully appreciated by the Russian authorities.

At that time, Prince Wittgenstein, struggling against Carolyne's divorce action, was doing everything in his power to
alienate Carolyne from Liszt, not only because of his own
relationship with her but because of his daughter Maria—
it was not proper, in his opinion, for her to grow up in the
Altenburg.

Agnes managed the first part of her assignment and even
partially succeeded in the second. Well trained by her father,
she knew the art of listening, which Liszt appreciated particularly because Carolyne talked almost constantly. During
his periods of self-doubt and discouragement, which Carolyne
interpreted as indolence, or when irritated by the provincial
attitude of Weimar, it soothed Liszt to find that Agnes
neither demanded anything from him nor ever reproached
him. "Thank you for your kindness, your tenderness and all
that grace of simplicity and inner poetry that captivates me,"
he gratefully repeated to her over and over again.

Nor did Liszt know that, in addition to her major task,
Agnes was to supply her father with information concerning
the political refugees whom Liszt met, even casually, on his
travels in Europe. Innocent of all this, he readily told her
their assumed names and addresses and information about
their secret activities.

Then, in 1855, Nicholas I died, and Prince Wittgenstein
had to seek new ways of reaching an agreement with Carolyne. Klindworth's usefulness was over. Without losing a
moment, because of the growing unrest in the political situa-

tion in Germany, he recalled Agnes from Weimar on the pretext of being ill and in need of her at home. At that time
Ferdinand Lassalle, the principal agitator and leader in the
labor movement, was living in Düsseldorf, and Klindworth
saw to it that while Liszt was staying with Agnes in the city
she would "accidentally" meet Lassalle, who was to be her
next assignment.

Because of Lassalle's leading role in the political turmoil
in Germany, Klindworth saw him as a useful source of information on international affairs—information that he could
pass on to the government authorities in Paris or London.
But Lassalle was an old hand at political intrigues. He had
a score of spies of his own, and he soon discovered what
Klindworth was up to. Although he often supplied father
and daughter with large sums of money, Lassalle was playing
his own game. While enjoying Agnes' charms, he managed
to get more information from her than she was ever able to
deliver to Klindworth.

No one was the wiser—Liszt least of all. Because Cosima
and Agnes were friends, Lassalle never breathed a word about
his relationship with Agnes to Hans von Bülow, or about
Agnes and her father's affairs in Weimar.

Liszt was nearing his fiftieth birthday, and he was very conscious of it. In fact, as if he believed that his life was ap-
proaching its end, he made an elaborate will, leaving most of
his possessions to Carolyne. Somehow he felt more indebted
to her than to Marie d'Agoult, although the strength of his
love for Carolyne had now abated, as always happened with
his infatuations.

During the second half of the 1850s, Carolyne was losing
her hold on Liszt. If he continued to work on his compositions at all, it was mostly because he felt indebted to her for
her "sacrifice." But after she had gone to Rome, his letters
to her complained of his depression, lack of energy, and

desolation at her absence. But he was repeating to Carolyne what in the past he had written to Marie—and to Agnes what he had written to Carolyne.

The truth of the matter was that his incredible energy was not his own. It had to be released by somebody else. Liszt

Liszt performing before Franz Joseph I, Emperor of Austria

had to be directed by another's discipline; his vanity had to
be flattered and his heart inflamed by the love of a woman.
But merely one woman was seldom enough.

Once again the independent bachelor, he resorted more
and more often to drinking. During his years with Marie

d'Agoult he had become used to smoking cigars and drinking coffee and tea in such large quantities that she grew alarmed for his health. But as soon as he started on his concert tours, which taxed his nervous system and physical resources during long, often uncomfortable travels, he needed much stronger stimulants. In addition to cigars and coffee, he drank wine, cognac and arrack (a kind of gin) in such amounts that by the time he met Carolyne a bottle of cognac per day was normal for him.

He knew well that his stomach trouble, bladder ailments and early-morning nausea were all caused by excessive indulgence, but he could not resist it. At the Altenburg, Carolyne regulated the quantity of liquor he drank. But now that he had no one to supervise him, he fell back into his old habits, and since even one glass of cognac went to his head, he was frequently under its influence by mid-morning.

Only when ill did he miss Carolyne's care. Now that she was close to getting her divorce, he shrank from the thought of marrying her—if he had ever considered this at all seriously. A mutual friend once ventured to warn him against marriage, saying, "You are not constant by nature, and you don't know what an unhappy marriage is." And Liszt replied, "I agree with you. What a man *has* experienced he knows, and that he can answer to. But what a man *will* do or not do, what he *will* feel, he cannot know, and to swear in this regard is a much more doubtful business. Who can take oath that he will always remain the same? I am certain that the best thing to do with me is always to leave me my freedom—it is dangerous to bind me either to one person or to one place."

In this last sentence he summed up his attitude about Carolyne and the thought of staying longer in Weimar. Having already embarked on the sea of romance, Liszt was in no hurry to join Carolyne in Rome, where she was sup-

posed to have been making final arrangements for their forthcoming marriage in the hope of returning to Weimar in a
more conventional position. The seventeen months of their
separation were fatal to their relationship and fatal for Liszt,
because they determined the course of the final thirty years
of his life.

He took trips to Vienna, Budapest and Berlin, where he
was sure to find acclaim and adulation, where he gave cham-
pagne parties for his admirers. He went to Paris, visited old
friends and was easily persuaded to play at the homes of
aristocrats. But the musicians—Hans von Bülow and Joseph
Joachim in Berlin, Clara Wieck and Robert Schumann in
Dresden, and even Wagner and Berlioz in Paris, all indebted
to him for his generous concern on their behalf—had turned
away from him. He was so used to keeping his opinions to
himself in Carolyne's presence, because he feared she might
disapprove of them, that now he could no longer be frank
and sincere. His extreme politeness sickened them.

In Paris he saw Marie d'Agoult again. Their conversation,
however, consisted of trivialities, although to please him she
gave a luncheon to which she invited several prominent men
in Paris society. And he exchanged only a few words with
Blandine—he was in a carriage on his way to an "important"
dinner party. He never saw her again. After giving birth to a
daughter, Blandine died in St.-Tropez seven months later,
in March 1860.

Taking his time, Liszt continued on his journey to Lyon,
Marseille, Nice and Naples. He finally arrived in Rome on
October 21, 1861, on the day before his fiftieth birthday,
which Carolyne was supposed to have chosen for their wedding—or so, at least, goes the story that has become part of
the Liszt legend.

Carolyne, we are told, after finally receiving her divorce,
made all the preparations for the ceremony. The Church of

San Carlo al Corso was decorated with flowers, and the event was to take place at six o'clock in the morning. One biographer has gone so far as to say that Carolyne "was an excited young bride despite her gray hair, and her ecstasy was moving and natural."

The story continues to the effect that Liszt and Carolyne spent the evening before at her apartment and retired at midnight because of the superstition which forbids a bridegroom from seeing his bride on the wedding day before they meet at the altar. Then a denouement worthy of a motion-picture melodrama took place. A messenger from the Vatican brought a sealed paper to Carolyne revoking her divorce until her case could be re-examined. Carolyne and Liszt accepted this interference in the legalizing of their union as ordained by God.

But the truth of the matter was that during their seventeen months apart Liszt had grown farther away from Carolyne than during his friendship with Agnes in Weimar. And while his letters still protested his undying love, his indifference to her after her arrival in Rome was too apparent for any woman to miss. Carolyne confessed later that, resigned to the inevitable, she never again even mentioned marriage to Liszt. He no longer needed her. She told him as much, and he agreed with her.

Carolyne was the second woman who should have been given Liszt's father's warning. "God knows what it has cost me never to see Woronince or Weimar again," she admitted later. Fanatically devout, she accepted her fate and spent the rest of her life writing on religious subjects, convinced that she was thereby bringing salvation to mankind. She never was an attractive woman. Now she grew stout and added multi-colored ribbons to her cap, because, she said, God desired her to wear the bright colors of happiness that are found in the rainbow.

Rome in the nineteenth century

In an apartment cluttered with green plants and flowers, behind heavy curtains that were drawn all day, Carolyne lay on her chaise longue in a haze of cigar smoke and did her writing by candlelight. Liszt visited her in the evenings, and occasionally a cardinal or a priest would join them. But his visits became rarer after Blandine's death, when he left his apartment at 113 Via Felice and moved to the little monastery of the Madonna del Rosario on the Monte Mario, thus beginning the sixth decade of his life in holy precincts.

PART IV

THE CLERIC

XI

*L*ISZT was offered his secluded abode by the Pope's librarian. Except for a Dominican priest and a servant, the cloister was deserted. His cell was furnished with a bed, a wooden work table that held a marble cast of Chopin's hand and a few books, and a small, old, out-of-tune piano. On the white-washed walls hung a dozen pictures of saints.

Yet even for an actor such as Liszt, it was impossible to renounce the world overnight. In the mornings he attended the priest's reading of Mass, but in the evenings he became restless and on one pretext or another went to the city, where he joined the company of less ascetic friends.

After six months of voluntary semi-exile, Liszt eagerly accepted von Bülow's invitation to a music festival in Karlsruhe, and in the first days of September 1864 he paid a visit to Weimar. A month later, however, he was back in Rome—and this time he seriously considered joining the priesthood.

Those who claimed to know about his personal affairs suggested two plausible reasons for his decision. Prince Nicholas Wittgenstein had died in March 1864, removing the last obstacle to a marriage between Liszt and Carolyne—a marriage, perhaps, that Liszt's sense of duty still bade him to see through. On the other hand, it was rumored that Carolyne herself, fearing that Liszt might be lassoed into matrimony

by a pretty though unworthy young upstart, induced the
Roman ecclesiastics to plant him in the church. But the
shrewdest observers suspected Liszt's idea of taking minor
orders as "only one of his bizarre stunts for the benefit of
the world—to make people talk about him."

Be that as it may, Liszt gave his "farewell" concert in the
Palazzo Barberini, where he played Weber's *L'Invitation à
la Valse* and his own arrangement of Schubert's *Erlkönig*.
The performance was enlivened as always by his old show-
man's trick of suddenly turning on his audience a carefully
calculated demoniac glance that bored into them like a
gimlet.

Then he retired to the monastery of the Lazzaristi in Rome
to prepare himself for his "calling." He rose at half past six,
meditated alone in his cell before breakfast, and afterward
attended Mass at half past eight. This was followed by solitary scripture reading, a visit to the Holy Sacrament and mid-
day dinner in the refectory, where he was placed alone at a
small table so far away from the others that he could not hear
what was read by a monk from the pulpit. After a siesta of an
hour and a half, he was subjected to more scripture readings,
walks in the garden, solitary meditation for an hour, and,
after a silent eight-o'clock supper, a talk with the superior
until half past nine. The lights went out at ten, and he had
to go to bed.

On April 25, 1865, Franz Liszt was tonsured in St. Peter's
at the hands of Cardinal Hohenlohe, the brother of Carolyne's son-in-law, Princess Maria's husband. Liszt received
four of the seven degrees of priesthood. He was now door-
keeper, reader, acolyte, exorcist, and an honorary canon, but
he could not celebrate Mass or hear confession. And if he
so desired he could leave the priesthood at any time.

A few days after the ceremony, Liszt was seen attired as
an abbé, his black silk cassock fluttering behind him as he

*A silhouette
of Abbé Liszt*

stepped from a hackney carriage. Was this, then, the end of
the *Don Juan parvenu?* Far from it.

Liszt was merely *disguised* as an abbé. For a while he
looked well and contented, but his new role did not satisfy
him for long. After all, he had given up acclaim and fame,
which in his more sober moments he considered to be nothing
more than a punishment for talent. Only six months passed
before he regretted the metamorphosis. For one thing, the
constant duel between spirit and flesh was affecting his appearance.

At fifty, after years of strenuous public life as a performer
and a private life just as exhausting, there were no traces left
of the handsome man of twenty years earlier. Strangers
meeting the composer for the first time now often spoke of
him as rather ugly, with hollow cheeks and deep lines on his
forehead, nose, mouth and chin, especially noticeable when
he was in bad humor. He looked old and shrunken and

smelled of tobacco. But for women, no matter what age, he still held an incredible fascination. Conscious of this, he could easily dismiss the fact that he made a disagreeable impression on men. Liszt never had a lasting friendship with a man, and to have a life that imposed on him exclusively male companions went against his nature and depressed him.

But this life was the price he had to pay for the fulfillment of composing music on religious subjects. To this period belong the *Deux Légendes: St. François d'Assise prédicant aux oiseaux* and *St. François de Paule marchant sur les flots*, and the oratorio *The Legend of St. Elizabeth of Hungary*, on which he began work in 1862. But, as if he wanted to prove that all his thoughts were not directed heavenward and that religious feeling had not completely supplanted his passion for less abstract subjects, he also composed at this time the *Mephisto Waltz* based on a scene in the Village Inn from Goethe's *Faust*.

In *The Legend of St. Elizabeth*, Liszt may have seen a parallel between his own life and that of his angelic compatriot, who loved heaven and sanctity above all and who, through her labors and charity, brought fame to the city of Wartburg—a city not far from Weimar, where Liszt himself generously donated gifts—but surely he did not fail to identify himself with Mephisto in *Faust*. The oratorio was eventually performed in Budapest, without much success, and it is now an almost forgotten work, while the *Mephisto Waltz*, one of the masterpieces among his piano compositions, remains to this day in the repertory of concert pianists.

After taking his orders, Liszt lived in the Vatican. His apartment adjoined that of Cardinal Hohenlohe, opposite the Loggia of Raphael, two steps from Michelangelo's Sistine Chapel. But after the Cardinal departed, Liszt moved to the monastery of Santa Francesca Romana with its unique view of the Forum and the Temple of Venus. Cardinal Hohenlohe also put at Liszt's disposal a suite of rooms in the Villa d'Este, built by Cardinal d'Este at Tivoli in the sixteenth century. Situated at the foot of the Tiburtian mountains, it rises above cascades of terraces among waterfalls and long alleys of cypresses.

Liszt had four small rooms and two servants there. He awakened every day at five in the morning and, dressed in an abbé's long one-button frockcoat and a bomba hat and holding a lantern in his hand, he walked over to the cloister for early Mass. He worked at his desk or at the piano most of the day. During Christmas week, shepherds playing bagpipes

Franz Liszt conducting The Legend of St. Elizabeth *in Budapest*

came down to the valleys with their flocks, and he invited
them in to visit him, ordered his servants to serve them
wine, and wrote down the melodies of their songs. But shepherds were not his only visitors. He was not content with the
company of the two young and pretty servant girls, whom he
liked to kiss, but received as well many beautiful women
from Rome—one of whom sent him camellias every day.

Whenever he had even more pleasant quarters offered him,
he declared that he had found, at last, the true El Dorado
for work "without interruption." Actually there was nothing
to hinder him from living the life of a priest or a monk, if that
was what he sincerely desired. But Liszt was not made for
martyrdom, and he could not resist the beckoning of the
world that he loved. In Budapest he enjoyed his old high life
with wealthy friends, in Weimar he had his studio, where he
was surrounded night and day by an enthusiastic crowd of
pupils, and at the Villa d'Este he found his own special kind
of retreat.

Liszt's teaching at Weimar benefited many fine pianists.
He took no money for his lessons—more often than not, he
assisted his students financially. The pose of the grand seigneur with the generosity of a prince was very important to
him—it was to be part of the legend about himself that he
was so anxious to create. And rather than run the risk of being
criticized for his goal he preferred to be grossly imposed
upon by his pupils.

If it had not been for Hans von Bülow, who assumed the
role of his guardian, Liszt would have had even less time than
he did have for himself and his work. From the ever increasing number of applications arriving constantly from all over
the world, von Bülow sorted out those worthy of the master's
attention. Eventually he had to have a printed notice pinned
to Liszt's door: "Not at home in the mornings. Out in the
afternoons."

The Monastery of Santa Francesca Romana in Rome

But until Liszt was much older and the mere physical exertion prevented him, he used to feel compelled to answer personally all the letters addressed to him, which amounted to some two thousand per year. Von Bülow was not always on hand to decide which of the letters deserved an answer. In the fall of 1869, while he was in Rome, Liszt received a letter begging him for lessons. He answered it with his usual comment: He was willing to teach "if your talent is worthy of encouraging." Liszt believed he was writing to a young man, but two weeks later, when his new pupil arrived, he was pleasantly surprised to see an attractive eighteen-year-old girl.

At their first meeting, Liszt realized almost instantly that the young lady knew nothing about piano playing, but she was so attractive in her fashionable white dress that he sought to console her for her long trip by sitting himself down at the piano and playing Chopin's *Polonaise in C sharp minor*.

He neither noticed her name nor asked anything about her,

and as if he were unaware of the emotions his playing had stirred in his visitor, he nonchalantly began to arrange the large bouquet of flowers she had brought him as he told her to come to his class on the following Friday afternoon.

At that session the girl was startled by the behavior of a large number of students and their parents and relatives. As Liszt entered the room they threw themselves upon him, covering his hands with long and unctuous kisses. Because she did not join this ritual, Liszt greeted her rather coldly and barely spoke to her during the lesson. But that evening, to her great surprise, he called at her apartment to apologize for his "rudeness" that afternoon, and, taking her head into his hands, kissed her forehead. He asked about her family and background and remained with her until very late listening to her story.

Olga Janina, referred to by Liszt biographers as a Cossack, was born a countess on her father's estate near Kiev, a city with which Liszt was already well acquainted because of his meeting there with Carolyne. Like the Princess, Olga came from a wealthy and noble family.

The large collection of weapons—Turkish yataghans, Arabian curved swords, long sabers with Damascus and Toledo blades, and Caucasian daggers—adorned the walls of her mansion and set the style for Olga's life, which was much less genteel than Princess Wittgenstein's. Whereas Carolyne as a young girl had read Voltaire and Goethe with her father, Olga at the same age was already an extraordinary horsewoman who, inspired by an old Cossack's stories of heroic exploits, spent her time hunting wolves or riding to death her father's pure Arabian stallions.

Closer to the Cossacks on the estate than to her parents, Olga had utter contempt for the wealthy class into which she had been born and genuine sympathy for the miserable lot of the peasants, her "vassals," who were, as she put it, "putrefying in mud and disease, ignorant even of the names of their fathers, and treated like beasts of burden and congenital idiots."

The "revolutionary" spirit burning in her heart "cried out" for her own liberty from home and her father's second wife, so that at the age of fifteen she married a man who soon after the ceremony revealed his real tyrannical colors. They separated after a few weeks. Her husband, taking her dowry and an additional large sum of money, gave Olga her freedom. Some months later, Olga gave birth to a daughter.

The story could have been Carolyne's, or Marie's.

But Olga was different from both women. She wanted to become a great pianist, an ambition she had acquired when, to console herself for the failure of her marriage, she began studying piano under the old director of the Conservatory in Kiev. This man had time to introduce her to some of Chopin's music and what was available of Liszt's, but then he died of gangrene caused by the bite of a tiger who was always at the side of one of the Cossacks on the estate. It was then, after losing her teacher, that Olga had written in desperation to Liszt imploring him to accept her as his pupil.

Of course Liszt's interest in Olga's ambition was immediately enhanced by the fact that she was an aristocrat, young, pretty and rich. He suggested that in the future he give her lessons on Tuesdays, alone, and at her apartment.

Olga was young, though not so young that she failed to recognize the actor in Liszt from the outset or see through the well-calculated wiles with which he was sure to conquer a newcomer—from the cold glance to the smile "that was like a shaft of sunlight." His pose of grand seigneur did not conceal a certain coarseness of nature, and his adulation of wealth and titles surprised and disgusted her even more than it had Countess Marie d'Agoult and Princess Wittgenstein.

But like Marie and Carolyne, and many others among his

Countess Olga Janina

female admirers, she soon fell in love with him, and she told him so.

Liszt took her in his arms and, after a long silence, said in a low voice: "Never speak to me of love. I must not love."

Olga need not have been brought up among the hot-blooded Cossacks to accept this obvious challenge. She would not let him dismiss a love that was, as she said, "as superb as the magnificent, fabulous Brazilian plant that flowers once only in a hundred years." And meaning every word of it, she resolved, "He shall be mine, or I will kill him."

For a while she kept away from Liszt, but she could not resist writing him, and upon his return from one of the out-of-town visits (to Munich, perhaps, where one of his "ad-mirers"—plain and old, but rich and titled—was known to live), Liszt came once again to see her.

"My answer to your letter is my return," he said. "I could not write. I ought not to love, but I do love and cannot con-ceal it. But I beg you," he added in a voice so caressing that it made Olga tremble from head to foot, "to have pity on me now that you have wrested this confession from me. . . . Please call me Ferencz." (Ferencz is a diminutive, endearing name for Franz in Hungarian.)

On the following day, however, he wrote her a letter begging her to love him, but to do nothing that might make him forget his duty or give him reason for shame and regret.

Olga knew what the next move must be. She took an apartment close to his, furnished it luxuriously to please the abbé's eye, and made a flying trip to Paris to equip herself with the most dazzling creations from the house of Worth, for Liszt had once told her that women could not wear too much lace, furs and jewelry for him. Then, sure of the effect she was going to produce among his guests, she appeared casually at one of Liszt's receptions at Santa Francesca Romana.

He introduced her to everyone, tenderly putting his arm around her waist. But Olga saw plainly that his affection was stirred by his flattered ego. A rich countess from the wild steppes of Russia, young and beautiful, was his latest conquest; had she been dressed more plainly he would not have even noticed her. Once again outrage at the basic sham of upper-class relationships filled her mind, but not her heart, which propelled her willy-nilly along the well-trodden path of love's progress.

For three months she refrained from seeing him alone, except when he gave her, or when she returned to him, the manuscripts he had entrusted her to copy because of her "superb handwriting."

Then, suddenly, she appeared on his doorstep at the Villa d'Este, interrupting his retreat. At first speechless, Liszt recovered himself and turned the key of his room. "I can no longer deny myself to you," he murmured. He took her into his arms.

On the following morning Olga became distressed. "He was mine," she reflected, "but when he awakens he will probably recoil from me and, weeping, take refuge at the feet of a crucifix, or he will seek out a priest and with his face in

the dust he will implore God's pardon for the crime of love,
which at the tribunal of penitence he will sully with names
of the most hateful kind."

Olga may have had a penetrating insight into his nature,
but she certainly overestimated the abbé's religious devotion
and underestimated her own charms. She was determined
to kill him before her fears were realized. In an instant she
had in her hand a small poisoned dagger, which she always
carried for emergencies. A thrust of this weapon would end
his life, then her own, for she was planning on joining him
"under the same winding sheet in the tomb, so that he would
remain hers for all eternity."

Liszt awoke and, perceiving with one half-closed eye the
dangerous blade pointed at him, spoke to Olga with as much
calm as he could muster. His first words of love lowered her
hand. He took her into his arms and, caressing her with
kisses, swore that he would no longer fight against his love.
Her fears quieted, Olga let the idea of killing him rest for
a while.

This romantic love affair was of shorter duration, but more
passionate, than those with Marie d'Agoult and Carolyne. In
contrast to the other women, Olga had no intention of being
left behind whenever Liszt took to his travels, and she either
went with him or joined him soon after his arrival at his
destination. She accompanied him to Weimar, where she
made herself even less popular than Carolyne, because she
could not restrain herself from expressing revulsion at the
behavior of Liszt's female entourage.

Olga, better than anyone else, witnessed the extent of the
foolish reverence paid to Liszt. The madness for mementos,
which included old cigar butts that had once rested between
the master's lips, was now surpassed by fights for drinking
what was left in his teacup or for carrying off in bottles the
used water from his washbowl.

The antics of his female admirers brought to a climax her irritation with Liszt, who was enjoying their conduct completely.

"These women are good," he tried to explain. "There is a striking thing about them that seems to escape your notice. All who know me are brought into sympathy with each other. *They love each other in me.*" If Liszt was suggesting that Olga join them, he might have been surprised by her reaction, which she wisely kept to herself: "Ah, Lord in heaven!" she thought. "Lord, you have been supplanted!"

A week before Easter of each year that they were together, Liszt would grow cold toward Olga, because he said the church had commanded him to repent. Resentfully, Olga once reminded him of his promise when faced with the blade of her dagger. "His eyes became veiled, he turned a timid glance toward heaven," she recalled later. Liszt spent the whole of the afternoons of Good Friday and the following day in church. On his knees before the image of Christ he poured forth tears in abundance and smote his breast. All Weimar wept in touching edification.

One Holy Week, Olga was alone in her rooms, cursing the church bells that seemed to rob her of her lover, when Liszt suddenly entered her bedroom. His radiant look and proud carriage were not appropriate to the season, but he had just completed one of his periodic repentances. Holding Olga in an ardent embrace, he whispered, "You see, my dear, there is nothing like putting your conscience in order." Never did a Christian celebrate better the resurrection of his Savior.

However, Olga soon discovered that Liszt was being unfaithful to her, and although she did not complain, he accused her of being jealous and "despotic," as he had often claimed of Marie and Carolyne, saying that their silence itself was a complaint. These trials were too much even for Olga's Cossack nervous system. She took to drugs, then fled to Paris and the Netherlands—but a letter from Liszt brought her back to him in Budapest, where he was staying. Apparently he could no longer live without her at his side. He proudly exhibited her to his wealthy friends and the Hungarian aristocrats who feted him. Olga was blissfully happy when, at the end of the year 1871, she learned from her banker that she was financially ruined.

"Liszt loved luxury," Olga remarked later. "He saw love only as surrounded by every refinement, every delicacy. He warmed only to rooms lit by alabaster lamps that exhaled perfumes; under his feet he needed soft white carpets; his eyes demanded the satisfaction of rare tropical plants." When she asked him what would happen to her if she ever lost her fortune, Liszt replied casually, "You would go and take an airing in your own country."

Olga tried to retrieve her money by gambling, but lost even her last penny. Bearing letters of introduction from Liszt, she went in desperation to the United States, hoping to earn some money as a pianist. But P. T. Barnum would not manage her career unless he could bill her as Liszt's daughter and unless she became his mistress. Olga would not consent to either.

She wrote frantic letters to Liszt, which at first he left unanswered, but he eventually replied:

The violence of your sentiments troubles the peace that is one of the conditions of my existence. Permit me therefore to forswear receiving your strange lucubrations until the time comes when you realize that happiness is possible only when one obeys the divine laws. You have to reconcile yourself to your fate, which indeed is the result of your many imprudences.

Olga was not willing to listen to this sermon from the old *Don Juan parvenu* in the abbé's cassock. In a boiling rage she sent him a one-sentence answer: "Monsieur, I am returning to

Franz Liszt at the piano

Europe to kill you." And she took the first boat to France.
Armed with two pills of *wourali*, which she obtained from
a friend who assured her that the poison would mean death

within six hours, she burst unannounced into Liszt's apartment in Budapest. To be fair to Liszt's talent for acting, it must be said that his seemingly calm demeanor almost fooled her. He tried to make love to her, but she would have none of it and called him a coward. He waved away the accusation by pointing out that despite her threatening letter he had remained in Budapest. She assured him that she was going to have her revenge, but not until the evening—she wanted the last few hours of the afternoon with him.

Liszt agreed, calmly rang for his servant and gave orders that no one was to be admitted for the rest of the day. But before the servant left the room, he handed his master an urgent letter. Liszt glanced through it and turned the message over to Olga. It was from a princess who was making her debut that evening in the theater and was pleading to see Liszt because she needed his encouragement. In her excitement Olga could not have been expected to detect the ruse, all planned since she had announced her threatening visit. "Go! I will wait for you," she said.

Where Liszt went remains unknown, but since Olga had sworn to pursue him to the ends of the earth, he made no attempt to escape her. He returned, and the two dined together. Then they were joined by several friends whom Olga suspected of seeing her last letter to Liszt. She remained until everyone had left, then produced the poison. Saying to Liszt that she intended one pill for each of them, she suddenly swallowed both.

Liszt fell on his knees and broke into prayer, though he followed it with sobs and protestations of love. He sobered up when Olga only laughed at him. He begged her to go and die in her own hotel, lest he be accused of a crime. Olga offered to write a note of suicide, but he was petrified by the thought of the inquiries and reports that would have to be made. "And my priest's robe!" he cried as he forced her to let him take her to her hotel.

He summoned a doctor, who persuaded Olga to tell him about the poison she had taken. But she refused to take an antidote until Liszt swore his eternal love for her on the medallion of St. Francis that he always wore next to his skin.

When she awoke at dawn on the following morning she was lying in Franz Liszt's arms. He had proven his love. But before he left her, Liszt felt compelled to say that his sentiments were still the same. "If I lied to you last night, it was because anything is justifiable to save a fellow being from suicide."

Olga succumbed to this last blow and left Budapest that very evening. Liszt never saw her again.

XII

*T*HE last decade of Liszt's life was no longer *Allegro con brio*, but *poco a poco piu piano a la fine*. He brushed aside with a "think nothing of it" the harassing episode with Olga, but after her he became more cautious in his amorous adventures. He no longer tempted himself with young women and instead invested the wealth of his still irresistible personality in the affections of the more sedate among his female admirers—the dividends were more comforting if less exciting. A list of the women who were ready to leave their husbands and children for Liszt, even when he was past seventy, would be too lengthy to recite.

"Liszt is too sensitive, too artistic, too impressionable to live without the company of women"—so spoke in unison those who loved each other in him. "He must have a number of them around him," one admirer observed, "just as in his orchestra he needs many instruments with various rich timbres." And, indeed, Liszt found such an ensemble in his class of students at Weimar.

Of course, he was not a magician and could not make musicians out of everyone who joined his class. Convinced that the majority would be more successful as *Hausfrauen* or, at best, as piano teachers for beginners, he tolerated them because of their "beautiful eyes," their "fine little hands" or their "voluptuous contours." He enjoyed flirting with the young and pretty when he joined them on their picnics in the woods near Weimar, but he was proud, too, of the young men such as Frederic Lamond from Glasgow, Alexander Siloti from Moscow, Moritz Rosenthal and Émile Sauer from Vienna, and a score of others who under his guidance were developing into "piano matadors," as he affectionately called them. Only for these students would he ever play his own compositions, which despite his advancing years and failing health he still could do dazzlingly. He refrained from public appearances, except on rare occasions for benefits of one kind or another. And if he played at them at all, it was never one of his own works. Nor did he care to have his orchestral pieces performed.

Liszt was bitterly disillusioned about his composing. Though he worked methodically even then, he had not written a single original work since his *Christus* in 1866. Making piano transcriptions of others' compositions, always as easy for him as writing letters, now occupied his time. He worked on these while traveling, in hotel rooms, when confined to bed with a cold, or in the early morning hours before going to Mass.

With his transcriptions Liszt developed public interest in compositions that otherwise would not have been easily heard. A great champion of contemporary composers and their works, he was particularly interested in the "Mighty Five," a group of composers who had founded Russian national music. Of the Five—Balakirev, Borodin, Cui, Rimsky-Korsakoff and Mussorgsky—he met only Alexander Borodin, who visited him in 1877.

Liszt, as the host, treated Borodin in princely fashion, entertaining him at luncheons and dinners and taking him to receptions at the Weimar court, at which he had remained welcome since his resignation. Liszt took him to rehearsals and concerts, insisted that Borodin assist at his piano classes, and devoted all his free time to discussions of the composer's and his compatriots' works.

Liszt surprised Borodin by his knowledge of all the major compositions of the Five, and Borodin was flattered by Liszt's sincere admiration of his own work. Liszt praised his *First Symphony*, saying that the first movement was perfect, that the andante was a *chef-d'œuvre*, and that the scherzo was enchanting. He went to the piano and played for Borodin from memory the passages that particularly impressed him. But above all he wanted to know how Borodin's work was re-

Interior of Liszt's study in Weimar

ceived in Russia, what his plans were, and whether he had a good publisher. He made Borodin telegraph his publisher for the score of his *Second Symphony*, and on the day after it arrived, Liszt gave the first performance of the work in Weimar.

Talking incessantly in French and German, Liszt caught Borodin's hand and held him pinned to the sofa for a long, detailed interrogation about everything musical that was going on in Russia. He asked about Rimsky-Korsakoff whom he esteemed very highly and whose *Sadko* he admired very much, despite the failure of its premier in Vienna. He wanted to hear about Balakirev. He pointed to Balakirev's *Islamey*, which was lying on his piano, saying that he played it himself and made his students study it. He wanted to know about Mussorgsky's *Boris Godunov* and regretted not having been able to hear its first performance in 1871.

He talked to Borodin about the essence of future music. "You know," he said, "in Germany they compose a great deal. I'm lost in a sea of music that threatens to submerge me entirely. But heavens, how flat, how insipid it all is! Not a single living idea! You and your friends in Russia are supplying the only vitalizing stream in contemporary music."

Borodin spoke of the views the Five held about the symphony. They thought it had reached its final development as a form of composition, thanks to Beethoven, Schumann and Berlioz. They considered the symphonic work based on the sonata form as outdated and favored the freer form pioneered by Liszt himself in his symphonic poems. The symphony, Borodin said, must no longer be constructed in four parts as Haydn and Mozart had conceived it a hundred years before. "The time has come for this to pass into oblivion, as well as the symmetrical and parallel construction within each movement. We have done away with all the academic forms —odes, speeches, statements, and even arias—in dramatic ex-

pression. Now the time has come to forget about the first
and second themes and the exposition—the *Mittelsatz* in
symphonic music," he concluded.

Liszt was gratified by Borodin's words, for he could only
agree wholeheartedly. Had he been teaching composition instead of instructing performers, these ideas could have been
the foundation of his doctrine in regard to future symphonic
music.

Finally, he and Borodin discussed Cui's *La Musique en
Russie*, a book that had been sent him by a mutual friend
because it contained a detailed analysis of the reform in opera
that the Russian national school was advocating. Borodin
explained that the Five believed opera to be still in a transi-
tional period, the third stage in its evolution. At the end of
the eighteenth century, opera, in the second stage, was still
regarded only as a vehicle for the display of vocal virtuosity.
The melody, the cantilena, was written not to suit the text
but to give the singers a chance to show off their voices. It
was Gluck who tried to restore opera to its original status as
a dramatic composition, but later composers like Rossini once
again made opera merely music for the concert hall, adorned
with scenery and costumes. The influence of Meyerbeer and
Weber in Europe and Glinka and Dargomijsky in Russia
was felt as opera developed further, but their efforts were
only partly effective.

So far, Liszt was in complete agreemnt with the views
of the Five, and he was anxious for Borodin to continue his
commentary.

"Then," Borodin went on, "suddenly a new reform came
in with Wagner. In this the Five joined, though fundamen-
tally they were opposed to Wagner's ideas." Their principles
were similar to those underlying the Wagnerian reform—it
was the means of implementing them that differentiated the
two schools of thought.

Alexander Borodin, 1833–1887

The Russians felt that the subjects of Wagner's operas had nothing *human* in them, that the works were personified abstract ideas that, like mannequins, were incapable of inspiring real interest. They believed themselves to be concerned with the human passions that charm and stir, confuse and trouble, the lives of men. Wagner, they charged, concentrated all his interest in the orchestra, stating his themes through the orchestra, while the singers had only fragments of recitative, which, if considered separately, had neither instrinsic value nor any precise meaning.

The Five insisted that the singers, the actors on stage, are there not solely to complement the orchestra but to create the action of the opera—the public watches *them*, listens to *them*, and it is therefore *they* on whom the principal interest should center. The Russians maintained that Wagner did his best to deny his characters all musical expression, that the vocal parts of his operas did battle with the orchestra just

to be killed by it, and that his musical ideas were swamped
by the heavy waves that roll one over the other, surcharged
with exaggerated harmonies and sonorities, hardly relieved
of monotony by a few beautiful pages.

They also objected to Wagner's invention of the *leitmotif*
that is tagged onto every character, even onto abstract ideas
like vengeance or objects like a sword. The mere mention of
the idea or the object causes the motif to pop up, as though
a spring has been pressed.

Although Borodin was aware of his host's loyalty to Wagner, he failed to restrain himself—he was much too passionate
in his beliefs for that. The Russians, he added, thought
generally that Wagner's doctrine was false, that though
Wagner was a composer of talent and individuality, he had
written more irritating music than good—some of it astonish-
ingly banal—and that the mad Wagnerian cult was more
fanatical than sincere.

Liszt, who was well known for his quick temper when challenged or criticized, and for his devotion to Wagner's works,
refrained chivalrously from interrupting his guest, who concluded his remarks by saying that the Russians attached little
importance to the erotic and the psychoanalytic—used to
such advantage by European composers, and, of course, Wagner—as sources of musical inspiration.

Perhaps Liszt felt inspired by his conversation with Borodin
to turn again to writing an opera. Or perhaps he felt that it
was too late, that he was too old for such a task. At the time
he said nothing about it to his guest.

Borodin's reference to the eroticism in Wagner's compositions may have brought to Liszt's mind his own attitude toward Wagner and a rift in their relationship that had only
recently been mended. Since he had first met Wagner, Liszt
had managed to admire the composer while closing his eyes
to the man's unattractive personal characteristics. Wagner's

private life was none of Liszt's business, but when it affected his own, he was bound to take another view.

Liszt had always claimed proudly that he had never seduced an innocent maiden or broken up a happy marriage. (Neither Marie d'Agoult nor Princess Wittgenstein were happily married when he entered their lives.) Thus he was more than dismayed when he learned that Wagner was capable of meddling with the seemingly happy marriage of Cosima and Hans von Bülow.

Von Bülow was as devoted to Wagner as he was to Liszt, so when Cosima, in 1864, after some seven years of marriage, decided to leave him for Wagner, twenty-five years her senior, von Bülow suffered a nervous breakdown.

Liszt found himself in an awkward situation: He was Cosima's father and a close friend of both men in the triangle. He rushed to a hospital in Munich to console von Bülow. He tried to persuade Wagner to relinquish Cosima, but he failed, and he broke off his relationship with them. Even when he read in the newspaper of their eventual marriage he made no attempt at reconciliation.

His enthusiasm for Wagner's works, however, was unflagging, and all that he did for them could fill a whole volume. So in spite of the personal differences that separated them, Liszt sincerely hoped that Wagner would invite him to the ceremony, scheduled for May 22, 1872, marking the laying of the cornerstone of the Festival Theater in Bayreuth. Wagner wrote Liszt, in a letter that reached him too late for him to attend the ceremony:

Cosima insists that you will not come, even if I invite you. Yet I am not willing *not* to invite you. Come! You entered my life as the greatest man to whom I have ever addressed words of friendship. You withdrew from me perhaps because you have less confidence in me than I have in you. . . . Through Cosima you are born for me a second time. . . . So you live in full beauty before

me in her. We are united beyond the grave. You are the first one
who, by his love, ennobled me. I yield now to a second and higher
existence through her to whom I am married, and I can now
accomplish what I could not have accomplished alone. Thus you
have become everything for me, while for you I remain unim-
portant. What an immense advantage you have given me over
yourself. And if I say, "Come," I mean by this, "Come home"—
for it is yourself that you will find here. May you be blessed and
beloved whatever your decision.

Liszt answered with similar flamboyance:

Dear and glorious friend: I do not know how to reply in words
to your letter, which has profoundly moved me. But I ardently
hope that the shadows and circumstances that have held me at
a distance will disappear and that we may soon see one another.
Then you will understand that my soul remains inseparable from
yours, revived in your "second and higher existence" in which you
are accomplishing what you "could not have accomplished alone."
I recognize there the grace from Heaven. The blessing of God
be with you both, together with all my love.

But almost six months passed before Liszt traveled to
Bayreuth to see Wagner and Cosima. "Let others judge and
condemn her," he said at last. "For me she remains a soul
worthy of the *gran perdono* of St. Francis and admirably my
daughter."

During the last twenty years of his life, Liszt traveled all
over Europe, no longer as a conqueror in pianistic fields but
as an honored guest at a variety of musical events. Not averse
now to performances of his own works, he crossed the Continent often to be present at each of these events.

In March 1866, he went to Paris, where his *Messe de Gran*,
commissioned by the Prince-Primate of Hungary for the con-
secration of the new cathedral in Gran in 1855, was to be
given at the church of St. Eustache. Almost one hundred
years before, Mozart's mother had been buried in the St.

Eustache cemetery, and Liszt saw in the church the com-
memorative tablet bearing her name. His own mother had
died on February 6, a month before his arrival in Paris. Although he was devoted to her, he had let many years pass
without seeing her. She had lived at the house of Émile Ollivier, Blandine's husband.

The *Messe de Gran* failed to impress even his former
friends, whom he later invited to air their criticisms. Berlioz
left the room while Liszt was still defending the merits of his
composition. Three years later, Berlioz died—but Liszt had not
seen him again.

Liszt outlived most of his old friends. Caroline d'Artigau
died in 1872, a loss that he felt far more than the death of
Marie d'Agoult. Four years later in Weimar, when he returned from one of his travels, he learned of Marie's death
in the papers, and a fews days later he received a letter from
Ollivier saying that she had died of pneumonia on March 5,
1876. Several months afterward he heard of the death of
George Sand. Although as active as ever, Liszt felt that it
was easier to die than to live.

He lived, however, to see his and Wagner's great dream
realized. On August 2, 1876, the Festspielhaus in Bayreuth,
Germany, opened its doors for performances of *Das Rhein-
gold* and, during the next three days, of *Die Walküre, Siegfried* and *Die Götterdämmerung*. Liszt led the procession of
"musical pilgrims" from all over the world. Ludwig II of
Bavaria, Wagner's close friend and patron, drove through
crowds of the curious along the flag-adorned streets of the
town. The Emperor of Germany with his daughter was expected to attend the performances, and the Emperor of
Russia and his cousin of Mecklenburg were staying with the
Duke of Württemberg. Princesses and princes, musicians and
poets crammed the hotels and the homes of the townspeople.

Later, at a banquet after the last performance, Wagner

closed his speech before some seven hundred guests by saying, "There sits the man who believed in me first of all,
when no one knew anything about me, without whom you
might never have heard one note of my music—my very dear
friend Franz Liszt."

The words fell pleasantly on Liszt's ears. He had never
forgotten Wagner's challenge, when he was an exile in
Zurich: "Let not the older man think of himself, but let him
love the younger through the love of what he can bequeath
him."

The two friends, the two great musicians of the epoch,
should have died at that banquet in the glamorous ambience
so dear to Liszt, in the light of triumph so desired by Wagner. But Wagner lived until 1883, and when the news of his
death reached Liszt in Budapest, Liszt said calmly: *"Lui
aujourd'hui—moi demain."*

The triumph at Bayreuth finished Liszt's relationship with
Carolyne, a relationship that had faded almost completely
as the years passed. Carolyne resented the fact that Liszt let
himself play second fiddle to Wagner—the role of a "super-
numerary," as she called it. "No one plays any roles here,"
Liszt replied. "One creates music and plays that."

Gradually Rome lost its attraction for Liszt, even though
Carolyne continued working there on the last part of her
twenty-eight-volume *magnum opus, The Inner Causes of the
External Weakness of the Church.* Liszt preferred to go to
Bayreuth instead, where he lived in a small apartment near
Wahnfried, Wagner's villa.

In April 1886 he went on a long journey that took him
eventually to England, where he had not been since 1841.
He attended several performances of his works, including
The Legend of St. Elizabeth of Hungary. This time the English paid high tribute to a great musician, and the festivities

organized in his honor were crowned with a reception given by Queen Victoria.

On his journey home to Weimar he caught a cold and grew very weak. A doctor from Halle diagnosed dropsy. But by the beginning of July, Liszt felt well enough to be present at the wedding of his granddaughter, Daniella von Bülow, in Bayreuth, and a week later, on July 19, he played at a concert in Luxemburg. This was the last time Franz Liszt played the piano. He returned to Bayreuth to hear *Parsifal* on July 23 and *Tristan und Isolde* two days later. His illness, however, developed into pneumonia, and he died on July 31, 1886.

Liszt's Hungarian friends wished his remains to be brought to Hungary, while other admirers thought that he should be buried either in Weimar or at the Villa d'Este. But he was buried in Bayreuth, in the garden back of Wahnfried, next

The Festspielhaus in Bayreuth,
completed in 1876 (Drawing by Kirchhoff)

to Wagner's grave, where his daughter Cosima was laid to rest in 1931.

Franz Liszt was at home everywhere, yet he was homeless. He belonged to various nations, and in his wide travels he acquired and made his own the traits and tastes of many other men. He kept abreast of all the intellectual trends of his time, though he never committed himself to any one of them. Of all the Romantics, he had the most romantic life and career, but in his heart he remained lonely. As a musician, he was a great instrument, but as a man he was sometimes out of tune. He fulfilled his ideas about music in his piano, vocal and symphonic works, but died a disappointed composer. As he often said, he believed in art as he believed in God. He believed in art's limitless progress, so long as the artist is not hindered by interference with his work. He believed in the future of music with all the strength of hope and of love.

SELECTED DISCOGRAPHY *

Note: The following list is drawn from recordings now available. Many records of the great performances by Liszt exponents are, unfortunately, out of print.

CONCERTO NO. 1 IN E FLAT MAJOR FOR PIANO AND ORCHESTRA
Gilels   *Bruno 14025*

Janis, Kondrashin, Moscow Philharmonic (*See also* Concerto No. 2 in A Major for Piano and Orchestra)
Mercury 50329 **90329**

Katchen, Argenta, London Philharmonic (*See also* Concerto No. 2 in A for Piano and Orchestra)
London 9193 **6033**

Kempff, Fistoulari, London Symphony (*See also* Concerto No. 2 in A Major for Piano and Ochestra)
Richmond 19023

Richter (*See also* Concerto No. 2 in A Major for Piano and Orchestra) *Philips 500000* **900000**

Rubinstein, Wallenstein, RCA Victor Symphony
Victor LM-2068 **LSC-2068**

CONCERTO NO. 2 IN A FOR PIANO AND ORCHESTRA

Janis, Rozhdestvensky, Moscow Radio Symphony (*See also* Concerto No. 1 in E Flat Major for Piano and Orchestra)
Mercury 50329 **90329**

Katchen, Argenta, London Philharmonic (*See also* Concerto No. 1 in E Flat Major for Piano and Orchestra)
London 9193 **6033**

Kempff, Fistoulari, London Symphony (*See also* Concerto No. 1 in E Flat Major for Piano and Orchestra)
Richmond 19023

* *Stereo recordings are listed in boldface.*

Richter, Kondrashin (*See also* Concerto No. 1 in E Flat Major for Piano and Orchestra) *Philips 500000*   **900000**

CONCERTO PATHÉTIQUE FOR PIANO

Vronsky and Babin   *Decca 9790*

DANTE SYMPHONY

Sebastian, Colonne Orchestra   *Urania 7103*   **57103**

FAUST SYMPHONY

Bressler, Bernstein, New York Philharmonic, Choral Art Society (*see also* Les Préludes, Symphonic Poem No. 3)
2-*Columbia M2L-299*   **M2S-699**

HUNGARIAN CORONATION MASS

Szecsödy, Tiszay, Simándi, Farago, Ferencsik
Deutsche Grammophon 18668   **138668**

HUNGARIAN FANTASIA FOR PIANO AND ORCHESTRA

Bolet, Irving, Symphony of the Air   *Everest 6062*   **3062**

Cherkassky, Von Karajan, Berlin Philharmonic (*See also* Hungarian Rhapsodies—Orchestra Versions; Mazeppa, Symphonic Poem No. 6)
Deutsche Grammophon 18692   **138692**

HUNGARIAN RHAPSODIES FOR PIANO

Horowitz (Nos. 2, 6)   *Victor LM-2584*

Horowitz (No. 19)   *Columbia KL-5771*   **KS-6371**

Janis (No. 6)   *Mercury 50305*   **90305**

Katchen (No. 12)   *London 9304*   **6235**

HUNGARIAN RHAPSODIES—ORCHESTRA VERSIONS

Von Karajan, Berlin Philharmonic (Nos. 4, 5) (*See also* Hungarian Fantasia for Piano and Orchestra; Mazeppa, Symphonic Poem No. 6)
Deutsche Grammophon 18692   **138692**

Silvestri, Vienna Philharmonic (No. 2)
Angel 35677   S-35677

MAZEPPA, SYMPHONIC POEM NO. 6

Von Karajan, Berlin Philharmonic (*See also* Hungarian Fantasia for Piano and Orchestra; Hungarian Rhapsodies —Orchestra Versions)
Deutsche Grammophon 18692   138692

Scherchen, Vienna State Opera Orchestra
Westminster   14101

MEPHISTO WALTZ

Kapell   *Victor LM-2588*

Rubinstein   *Victor LM-1905*

MISSA SOLEMNIS (GRAN FESTIVAL MASS)

Ferencsik, Budapest Orchestra
Deutsche Grammophon 18646   138646

PIANO MUSIC

Darré—"Valse oubliée," "Campanella," "Sonetto 123 del Petrarca," "Feux follets," "Harmonies du soir" (*See also* Sonata in B Minor for Piano)   *Vanguard 1150*   71150

LES PRÉLUDES, SYMPHONIC POEM NO. 3

Bernstein, New York Philharmonic (*See also* Faust Symphony)   *2-Columbia M2L-299*   M2S-699

Von Karajan, Philharmonia Orchestra
Angel 35613   S-35613

SONATA IN B MINOR FOR PIANO

Darré (*See also* Piano Music)   *Vanguard 1150*   71150

Gilels   *Victor LM-2811*   LSC-2811

Horowitz   *Angel COLH-72*

SONGS

Fischer–Dieskau (in German)
Deutsche Grammophon 18793   138793

PICTURE CREDITS: Art Reference Bureau, Inc. (Photo Bulloz), 4; The Bettmann Archive, 5, 18, 22, 32, 51, 66 (top), 76, 81, 119; Culver Pictures, 2, 25, 39, 61, 95, 103 115, 123, 136, 139; The Granger Collection, 8, 10, 43, 56, 121, 131; Historical Pictures Service—Chicago, 13, 21, 40–41, 46, 69, 72, 84, 90, 107, 110–111, 145; Music Collection, New York Public Library, 66 (bottom), 98, 99; Roger-Viollet Agency—Paris, 16; Société "Frédéric Chopin" —Warsaw (Courtesy of the Polish Embassy, Washington, D.C.), 27, 48. Picture research by Patricia Crum.